The Divine Comedy of Sales:

The Sales Manager's Guide to Virtuous Leadership

Matthew McDarby

Eaton Press
We make your book happen

This book is dedicated to the most honest and forthright sales leader I've ever known, John G. McDarby, and to the memory of Monsignor Thomas Wells.

Table of Contents

Introduction

Whether you are a first-time sales manager or a veteran leader, you likely deal with some common problems that other sales managers face on a regular basis. In my first two books, I addressed two of the most common and most difficult problems, offering stories to illustrate how top sales leaders I've observed were able to overcome them.

In *The Cadence of Excellence: Key Habits of Effective Sales Managers*, I addressed a problem that all sales managers face at some point in their career as leaders—no time to do important things well. In that first book, I share stories and some practical ideas about how to establish and maintain the right sales operating rhythm with your team, increase your coaching effectiveness, build a coaching culture, align sales with your go-to-market strategy, and establish the discipline of planning. If any of those topics resonate with you now, I would be honored if you would pick up a copy of

The Cadence of Excellence on Amazon.

In *The Ultimate Differentiator: The Sales Manager's Guide to Talent Development*, I offered an approach to the talent problem facing sales organizations today, particularly for those organizations that depend on their field sales force to differentiate from the competition. In this book, I offer a practical and systematic way of looking at sales talent development that is a departure from the way sales managers historically have thought about recruiting, hiring, on-boarding, and managing performance. If this is an area where you have some struggles and want some simple and practical guidance, *The Ultimate Differentiator* is available on Amazon now.

The problem that I will address in this book is just as common and perhaps more insidious as the *time* and *talent* issues I've written about before. It affects every sales manager in some form or fashion. I am referring to the sales leader's *mindset*—specifically, establishing and maintaining the kind of mindset that great sales leaders leverage to build real followership and consistent, positive, and sustainable team results.

The American Heritage Dictionary of the English Language defines **mindset** in the following way:

Mindset (n)
- A fixed mental attitude or disposition that predetermines a person's responses to and interpretations of situations.
- An inclination or a habit.
- A way of thinking; an attitude or opinion, especially a habitual one.

What is the "fixed mental attitude" or "way of thinking" that great sales leaders apply to get their teams to follow their strategy, to be motivated, to fight through the challenges of modern selling to deliver great results? What separates the leaders who are able to lead their teams to generate consistently great results from those leaders who cannot?

In this book, we will take a look at sales leadership mindset through the lens of the people being led. What are the qualities of the sales leaders you would be inclined to follow? What actions do they take that makes them attractive leaders? What are the key behaviors that separate them from their average counterparts?

While thinking about categorizing the various ways that a great sales leadership mindset is different than the average leader's mindset, I found it simpler to identify the negative aspects of the human mindset than to identify the positive ones. Why is that?

Like most professional salespeople, I've had great sales managers and some not-so-great sales managers. The common thread among those who were not-so-great was that they clearly did not think about their role the same way a great leader would. The simplest way for me to describe their way of thinking is to use words like selfish, arrogant, rude, and shortsighted, but I needed a better way to organize and describe the mindset of those sales leaders who I did not want to follow.

Then, it hit me . . . the framework already exists. My mind raced back to junior high school and an acronym I learned from my brilliant English teacher with the Irish brogue, Patricia Fagen, or "Miss" as she would often ask us to call her. "Miss" Fagen wrote the acronym on the board in yellow chalk—"PEISAGL."

I can't recall if we were reading Dante's *The Divine Comedy* or if it was another very old volume that we were studying at the time, but **PEISAGL** is etched in my memory:

Pride, **E**nvy, **I**re, **S**loth, **A**varice, **G**luttony, **L**ust

PEISAGL—These are the seven deadly sins. Every human is

prone to them, and to varying degrees, they affect how we look at ourselves, how we treat others, and the choices that we make every day. Sales leaders have to contend with the seven deadly sins just like everyone else, but they may be particularly prone to them given the importance of their role in a business and based on the types of people who gravitate toward sales leadership roles.

My theory: If we allow the seven deadly sins to influence our mindset, we become less attractive, less influential, less likely to build trust or followership, and less likely to perform at peak levels. Conversely, a mindset guided and influenced by the great virtues is likely to make us more attractive to others, more influential, more trustworthy, and more likely to reach our full potential.

Who wouldn't want that? What sales leader wouldn't want that?

I did some research to remind myself where I first learned about the seven deadly sins. Dante's *The Divine Comedy* is divided into books, and the second book, "Purgatorio" or "Purgatory," is based on the seven deadly sins. I will summarize them here because I imagine you are not leaping out of your chair to pick up your desk copy of *The Divine Comedy* right now.

The seven deadly sins are as follows:
- Pride
  - A feeling of deep pleasure or satisfaction derived from one's own achievements, the achievements of those with whom one is closely associated, or from qualities or possessions that are widely admired
  - Pleasure, joy, delight, gratification, fulfillment, satisfaction, sense of achievement, comfort, contentment
- Envy
  - Painful or resentful awareness of an advantage enjoyed by another joined with a desire to possess the same advantage

- Jealousy, covetousness
- Ire
  - Strong vengeful anger
  - Anger, rage, fury
- Sloth
  - Disinclination to action or labor
  - Laziness, sluggishness, apathy
- Avarice
  - A selfish and excessive desire for more of something (e.g., power or money)
  - Greed, cupidity
- Gluttony
  - Excessive indulgence
  - Piggishness, excessiveness
- Lust
  - Urgent desire or interest
  - Desirousness, appetite

Standing in opposition to the deadly sins are the great virtues, otherwise known as the lively virtues. They are both the antonyms and the antidote to each of the deadly sins, and are as follows:

- Humility
  - The quality or condition of being humble, not proud or arrogant
- Goodwill / Gratitude
  - Benevolence; kindness
  - The quality or feeling of being thankful
- Calmness / Patience
  - Free from agitation
  - Quiet, steady perseverance; even-tempered
- Liveliness / Diligence

- o Vivaciousness, full of life
- o Constant and earnest effort to accomplish a goal
- Generosity
  - o Readiness in giving; freedom from meanness or smallness of mind
- Moderation / Self-control
  - o Avoiding extremes or excesses; temperance
  - o Control of one's actions, feelings
- Detachment
  - o Not attached, impartial or objective

As you read that list, which of those deadly sins jumped off the page? Which ones struck you as being most closely related or connected to a poor sales leader's performance?

Which of their antonyms struck you as most closely connected to a great sales leader's performance?

The answers to those questions are exactly what we will explore in this book. We will also take a very practical and useful dive into how to avoid the deadly sins as a sales leader and to apply their antonyms—the great virtues—to your role. At the end of this journey together, we will be very clear about the mindset and the behaviors that will propel you to the ranks of **consistently great** sales leaders.

Presuming you are up for that journey (because you are reading this book), let's dive into the seven deadly sins of sales leadership. We will do so by considering some stories of real-world leaders, and we will examine how the deadly sins played out and affected them, their teams, and their results. We will also consider stories of great leaders who made a different choice, eschewing a deadly sin in favor of a virtuous approach to leading their teams. The results of the choices made by the sales leaders I tell you about in this book will illustrate the stark difference between leading with virtue versus the opposite.

This book is not meant to be a victory lap for me or a wagging finger aimed at my less than virtuous colleagues in sales leadership roles. I am on this journey as well, battling the seven deadly sins each and every day, working toward being a more virtuous leader. Because I am human, it is not realistic for me to think I will reach a state of perfect virtue, but I can certainly try. It is in the trying that I will demonstrate more of the right behavior to the people I coach, develop, and lead, and it is in the trying that I will have the proper orientation and the right mindset to do the job of sales leadership just like the best performers do. I believe that is why this journey is going to be worthwhile for you, as well.

As we dive into each of the virtues and how they apply to your reality, I will offer some simple ways of thinking about the virtues, how they fit together, how they impact you, and how they impact your team.

The seven great virtues fall naturally into two simple categories that illustrate their orientation and impact on a sales team:

How I Carry Myself (Self-Orientation)

- Humility
- Calmness, patience
- Liveliness, diligence
- Moderation, self-control

How I Treat Others (Other-Orientation)

- Goodwill, gratitude
- Generosity
- Detachment

Self-Oriented
- Humility
- Patience
- Diligence
- Self-Control

Other-Oriented
- Goodwill
- Generosity
- Detachment

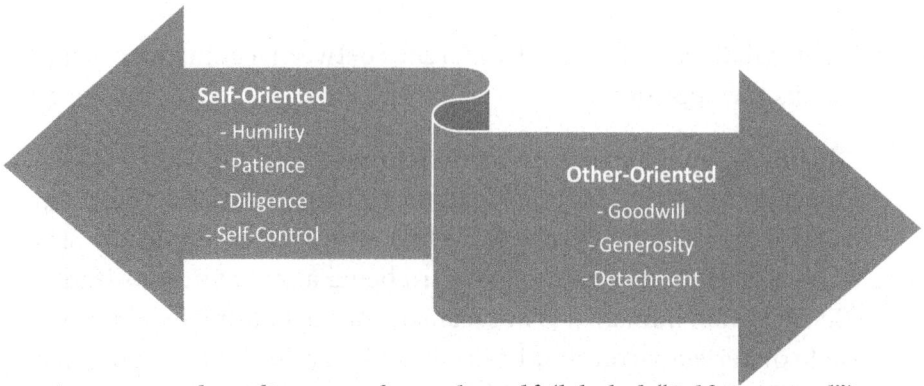

The virtues that align mostly to the self (labeled "Self-Oriented") have immediate impact on how a sales leader carries herself or himself. The virtues that align mostly to others (labeled "Other-Oriented") have immediate impact on how a sales team is treated by its leader.

In the next ten chapters of this book, I will note how each of the virtues specifically impacts you as a leader and/or your salespeople, clients, and colleagues. In this way, I will make clear connections between the virtues and their very real impact on your everyday life.

"The modern world is not evil; in some ways the modern world is far too good. It is full of wild and wasted virtues. When a religious scheme is shattered . . . it is not merely the vices that are let loose. The vices are, indeed, let loose, and they wander and do damage. But the virtues are let loose also; and the virtues wander more wildly, and the virtues do more terrible damage. The modern world is full of the old Christian virtues gone mad. The virtues have gone mad because they have been isolated from each other and are wandering alone."

—*G. K. Chesterton*

"Pride makes us artificial, and humility makes us real."

—*Thomas Merton*

Chapter One

Pride Goes Before the Sales Team's Fall

The trouble with pride is that it is a two-edged sword. We take pride in our work. We are proud of our accomplishments, our children, our teams, and that is all good. To take pride in what you do as a leader is important, as it serves to motivate you to do your very best at the work of leading.

But there is a dark side to pride, and that is why it tops our list of the seven deadly sins. Pride can cause us to turn our attention inwardly in an unproductive way, focusing on ourselves and what makes us great or desirable. Pride can be terribly problematic for a sales leader who seeks to build a team with great comradery and commitment. People who work for extremely prideful leaders tend to be less committed to the mission and less motivated to developing their own capabilities. To illustrate my point, I would like you to consider a few simple stories.

Stacking the Presentation Deck

I recently had the chance to speak with Malcolm Simmonds, a very successful senior executive in the food service industry. Earlier in his career, Malcolm was the chief customer officer for a major, global food service firm. He rose to that role based on his skills and his reputation as an inspirational leader who had a track record of building high- performing teams.

He told me about a situation in which pride, specifically the pride demonstrated by those in senior leadership roles, had a seriously detrimental effect on the morale and the performance of members of the sales and delivery organization. When speaking about his experience in his Chief Commercial Officer role, he said, "There was a definite bias to over rotate on how things looked (e.g., PowerPoint decks) versus customer value activities." Members of the executive team frequently intervened to rewrite presentation decks that had been prepared by salespeople, and often, their reasons for doing so were unclear to the sales team.

"I distinctly recall an example when we were preparing to see [a major fast-food chain] for a first sales call, and everyone on the leadership team wanted to put their fingerprints on the presentation. We actually delayed the customer meeting several weeks while executives made changes to the presentation."

They felt their contributions to the deck were more important than keeping to their schedule with the client. "Ultimately, we didn't sell them anything, and we lost the chance to even have a dialogue because management didn't feel comfortable having a capabilities discussion. It was believed to be showing too much vulnerability. But the deck was awesome!"

In this case, pride takes the form of the executive(s) needing to be right, even if their need to be right is in conflict with what is actually the right thing to do. As leaders, we must ask ourselves,

"Do I really need to put my fingerprints all over this deck (or this meeting or this project) and make sure it is 'right' according to my own standards? Or would we (or our team or our client) be better served by letting someone else work at getting it right?" There are times when there is only one answer, one way to skin the proverbial cat, but in my experience working in B2B sales, there is often more than one way to get the outcome we want. In the worst scenarios I've personally experienced, the prideful leader gets in the way of the desired outcome because he has to be right. The message that the prideful leader sends to his team is: "I don't trust you to get this right. Only I can do it."

The impact that unspoken message has on a team's motivation level and commitment is predictable, and it is not positive. I've seen and experienced this firsthand more than once over the years. The team's reaction, though typically unspoken, is some version of, "If you don't trust us, then do it yourself. We don't care."

Humility Over Pridefulness

When we see others—our salespeople, our colleagues, our clients, our partners—we know that each person matters and has intrinsic, God-given worth. We treat them with respect and dignity, and far more often than not, they reciprocate. If your intention is to build a team or to build strong relationships with clients and partners based on mutual respect and dignity, then humility is the virtue that you must apply in hefty measure.

What does it look like to function with great humility as a sales leader? What happens when we choose humility over pride?

A friend and past client of mine, Dana Isola, told me a story about his personal experience and the professional impact of choosing humility over pridefulness.

Several years ago, there was an open regional manager position in the northeast region where Dana was a part of the sales team. At that stage in his career, he was a top national producer, and he was also the region's go-to person in terms of strategic sales advice and clinical guidance.

Dana's goal was to be recognized as the leader he thought he was, but his self-perception did not match up with how he was perceived by others. Dana had been a top producer for four straight years, and he became the go-to resource for other team members when they needed clinical guidance and sales advice.

"To my surprise, I was not even considered to interview for the job. The job was awarded to someone outside the company that by all accounts was a good candidate. From my immature standpoint, he was not as qualified to handle the job as me. That opinion was based on the fact that the team was already looking to me for leadership and coaching, and I had a strong understanding of our business and how to execute at a high level. With that being said, I had no sales leadership experience or training, and my version of leadership did not match up with what others wanted from me."

"As a man of faith," Dana continued, "I took great pride in how I treated others and conducted myself in and out of work. With that said, we all have weaknesses, insecurities, and blind spots."

When we recognize our own blind spots, that gives us an opportunity to choose to grow into a better version of ourselves.

Dana said, "Being passed on this opportunity led me down a dark road with a very bright ending."

Dana approached his manager, Jeff Larson, an area vice president at Medtronic at the time, and they scheduled a meeting to talk about why Dana was not considered for the regional manager job. "I wanted Jeff to explain to me why I was not considered," Dana said. "For some crazy reason, I thought they would admit a mistake. Maybe they would say they didn't know I was serious about leadership and that I would be considered for the next job.

"The meeting finally came, and I had my chance to speak to Jeff. It did not go as planned! Jeff sat back and listened to me ramble about who I thought I was, what I did for the team, and why they made a mistake not considering me for the job.

"Jeff's first response was, 'Dana, you are a great clinical resource to your team.' Jeff is a master with words. He knew that comment would get a rise out me. He knew how I would respond; he knew where to take the conversation to wake me up to reality. After I was done letting him know how demeaning his comment was to me, he asked me a few direct questions that cleared things up quickly.

"He asked me, 'Dana, when was the last time a leader outside your area called you for advice? When was the last time a leader from outside your immediate area called you to help coach up a rep that is struggling? When was the last time someone at corporate called you onto a small group of select people to build an initiative?'"

Jeff then detailed other events from the past, and he asked Dana how he thought those actions impacted others around him.

"I will never forget how I felt in that moment," Dana said. " I was humiliated because I finally realized how far off my self-perception was versus reality and how my actions were impacting others. I realized this was not the man I wanted to be, this was not how I wanted to treat others, and that my actions were not in line with my beliefs or expectations for myself."

Dana realized he was looking at himself through a blurred lens. That lens was blurred by pride.

Jeff wrapped up the conversation by giving Dana some praise. He explained to Dana that his voice had great weight among the sales force. Jeff gave examples of the times that Dana used his passion and knowledge to better the company, and he pointed out how others naturally followed Dana.

"He told me I have a gift to create followership that not many have, and when used properly, could accomplish great things," Dana said. "He explained that I needed to use self-awareness around why decisions were made, who may have been involved, and how I can help drive success in all circumstances once a final decision was made. I gave him my full commitment to be the best sales leader in the company, and I would exceed even the greatest expectation he could have had for me."

This moment was a turning point in Dana's life and in his career.

"I could have dismissed the feedback, but instead I used it as a great source of power to become the best version of myself. I knocked on my regional manager's door that night and apologized to him for everything I did to disrupt what he was trying to build. I took full ownership of everything. I told him from that morning forward, I would help him execute the strategy and get buy-in from the team, and he was going to improve my ability to become the best leader I could be. We were unstoppable from that point forward."

That same year, Dana was asked to join several important committees at Medtronic. He was asked to travel the country to help under-performing reps reach their potential. He did all this while setting the company's sales growth record, becoming the first and only person to grow sales by $1 million in a single year. The following year, Dana was promoted to regional manager, made some great hires, and kicked off a long streak of high performances by his team.

"The whole experience made me feel better about who I am," Dana said. "I have a servant sales leader mentality to my core, and as a leader, I serve my people, keep them engaged, and have their best interests at heart. I've promoted a lot of people over the years because of that."

To be exact, Dana has successfully promoted six members of his team to important roles—three became district managers, one a clinical sales manager, one a key account manager, and one a senior training manager. He has trained and coached dozens of sales managers, and he has trained and helped hundreds of sales reps both domestically and globally.

This "awakening," as Dana describes it, became a great lesson that he was able to share with other, high-potential reps who wanted to be leaders. For those who were on the wrong path, who looked at themselves through a prideful lens, Dana's story was not only relatable but served as a compass to help them find a new course.

"I had a choice. I could have rejected the tough feedback that Jeff gave me and left to take a job somewhere else," Dana said, "but I chose the better path."

Learning, growing, sharing, being curious, listening, and helping all stem from our humility. As Dana put it, "God made us all unique and gave us unique perspectives. We all have something of value to offer."

The people we are responsible for helping and developing have unique capabilities, strengths, know-how, and experiences. We must approach coaching situations, for example, with humility if we want to add value and influence others. It's as true in coaching and leading as it is in the act of selling. We cannot let our pride get in the way.

In short, selling isn't about me, and neither is leading. If I allow my pride to make myself the center of the universe, then I am repellant to my team and to my clients. All that is truly great and effective about my work is obscured, and I am not able to create the sort of environment for my team or for my clients that I want to create. Trust is diminished. Value is eroded, and ultimately, my pride gets in the way of the kind of life that I want to lead, both in and outside my work life.

Practical Humility

How do we manifest humility while leading a sales team?

The answer is relatively simple: Be more focused on the other. By "other" I am referring to your sellers, your clients, your partners, and your colleagues. It is not only possible but quite practical to incorporate an other-focused approach when leading, coaching, selling, and collaborating. One very simple way is to ask a very other-focused question:

What are you trying to achieve?

What are you trying to achieve, Ms./Mr. Seller? How can I help you get there? If you achieve your goals, only then can I achieve mine!

What are you trying to achieve, Ms./Mr. Buyer? What is the outcome you want to achieve? What are you doing to achieve it? What's hard about that? Does that also mean you're unable to do X, Y, and Z? Are you looking for a way to achieve that? Can I share some ways in which I/my team have helped others achieve something similar?

What are you trying to achieve, Ms./Mr. Partner? How can we help you get there? What goals do we have in common? How can we help each other?

What are you trying to achieve, dear Colleague of mine? Do we have a shared vision of success? Do you have obstacles that I can help you overcome?

These brief examples of dialogue between a sales leader and a seller, a client, a partner, and a colleague all sound very simple, and that is because they are simple. Why don't we have this very simple conversation with our most important constituents?

Because our pride makes it harder than it needs to be. Pride inserts the phrase, "Let me tell you about me and what I want," before all of those simple conversations begin.

Read the following statement as if you were a potential customer: *Let me share a bit about me/my company, and then we'll talk about what you're trying to achieve.*

How important am I making you feel right now? What if I were your leader? Where do you think you stand in my pecking order? As a partner, whose agenda do you think I want to pursue, yours or mine? As a colleague, do you believe I have your best interests at heart?

When we allow our pride to inform the agenda, putting ourselves first in our thoughts and in our conversations with others, we leave those others with a negative impression. They come to the conclusion that we don't care about them as much as we do ourselves, and that erects a huge barrier to building trust and creating value. Knowing how critical strong relationships are for a sales team's success and a business's success, we must eliminate prideful leadership and prideful selling. If you want to strengthen your relationships externally and internally, a good dose of practical humility is going to be a crucial component of that plan.

In the introduction, I categorized humility as one of the "self-oriented" virtues, meaning that this virtue primarily impacts the way you carry yourself. True humility in practice forces us to look at ourselves differently—not to look at ourselves in a negative way or to downplay our value to others. Instead, looking at ourselves through the lens of humility gives us a realistic sense of our role in others' lives and the degree to which we can affect their actions, attitudes, and motivation. In this way, looking at ourselves humbly sets us in the proper mindset to help others commit to actions that will lead to their success.

If you've concluded there is room for at least a little bit more humility in the way you approach your work as a sales leader, then take the next logical step. Commit in writing to how you will go about incorporating more humility in your work life.

I've used the Start, Stop, Continue device in my other two books and in dozens of client engagements because it is a simple way of identifying incremental steps you can take on the path to making important changes. At the end of each chapter in this book, I've included a Start, Stop, Continue exercise with questions designed to help you consider ways you can accelerate the virtues and avoid the deadly sins in your work life. Take a crack at the Start, Stop, Continue exercise for this chapter now.

Start, Stop, Continue exercise

What can I do right now to inject some practical humility into my relationships with my sellers? With clients? With partners? With my colleagues?
What must I stop doing to avoid giving others the impression that my agenda comes first?
What should I continue doing to demonstrate an appropriate amount of humility as I lead my team? As I communicate with clients? As I work with partners? As I collaborate with colleagues?

"Joy is a sign of generosity."

—*Mother Theresa*

"Leadership must be based on goodwill. Goodwill does not mean posturing and least of all, pandering to the mob. It means obvious and wholehearted commitment to helping followers."

—*Admiral James Stockdale*

Chapter Two

Envious Leaders Take Their Team Astray

How does envy manifest itself in the context of business and sales, specifically?

Personal envy or jealousy can certainly rear its ugly head within a sales team, especially when that team comprises people who are naturally competitive, who want to be the best. If you want to be the best, that means you have to be better than someone else. If you're that someone else who is being bested, you may harbor some ill will, or go so far as to point out that top performer's good fortune, better leads, richer territory, or the preferential treatment he or she receives from management. To find envy running rampant within a sales team is quite common.

Some leaders unintentionally allow envy to run its course within their team, and internal relationships, camaraderie, and team morale suffer because of it. Other leaders stoke envy, using jealousy as a sort of driver of the behavior they want. After all, don't we want sellers who are fueled by the desire to be the best? Perhaps so, but there is a point where jealousy reaches an unhealthy level on a team and impacts relationships internally and externally.

Jealousy Between Leaders

I'm reminded of a story from one of my first engagements as a sales leadership coach and advisor. I was working with a mid-market company that had two sales leaders, one responsible for direct sales and the other responsible for channel and partner sales. Both leaders were incredibly smart and talented sellers, and they had risen through the ranks from individual contributors to leaders of the two key sales functions within their company. Over the years, however, some jealousy developed between these two leaders, as they competed more than once for promotions, for recognition, and for power on a leadership team that had seen a great deal of change over the course of their tenure with the company.

Despite these executives' attempts to hide their jealousy of one another, it was apparent to me, to other members of the leadership team, and to members of their respective parts of the sales organization that the professional jealousy they harbored for one another had degenerated into a lack of trust and transparency.

A perfect way of illustrating how jealousy affected their relationship in a very real and noticeable way was how they handled something as essential as reporting and information sharing. Though they handled different parts of the sales function, both of these leaders were responsible for sharing insights into clients, the marketplace, and competitors, as these were critically important for the leadership team to understand. Rather than collaborate and put their best insights forward together, they competed with one another, hid information from each other, and at times, presented wildly different perspectives on the market simply because they would not bother to compare notes, share ideas, or open themselves up to one another.

Being in a highly competitive market, the company's leadership team depended heavily on those insights to shape the company's product strategy, marketing effort, sales strategy, headcount, structure, and so forth. Because the two key sales leaders were unwilling to help one another out of jealousy, the business and its sales results suffered. On top of that, the two sales leaders suffered reputational damage within the executive leadership team and across the organization. In short, everyone in the organization had doubts about the two executives' leadership capabilities because of the way they treated one another and let their professional jealousy get in the way of the important work they could have been doing together.

In this altogether too common example, we can see clearly how professional jealousy or envy can impact an individual leader's relationship with others and with his or her team, and how it can ultimately affect the entire business. Jealousy might cause people to shade the truth about another member of their team, to put themselves first above others, and to take actions that erode trust. I think we can safely say that none of those behaviors are desirable in a sales organization.

Goodwill and Gratitude

The opposites of jealousy and envy are goodwill and gratitude. The *Merriam-Webster* definition of *goodwill* includes "benevolent interest and concern." We can also interpret the word to mean "willing the good of the other" (hence, "good" and "will"). By demonstrating that we "will the good of the other" and that we are grateful, not resentful, for the problems and opportunities we have to address, we create the sort of environment where trust is created, and collaboration is not only encouraged but enabled.

How can you instill a culture of goodwill and gratitude as a sales leader? And when is it critically important to do so?

I wrote about a great sales leader I've come to know in my second book, *The Ultimate Differentiator: The Sales Manager's Guide to Talent Development*, and his name is Ken Napolitano. Ken is currently the chief sales officer (CSO) at WheelsUp, a fast-growing (you might say "high-flying") player in the private aviation business. Ken and I spoke recently about his experience at WheelsUp, and it is a great story about how a leader who focuses on building and maintaining goodwill can solve even the most complex problems in a sales organization.

A key part of WheelsUp's growth strategy is mergers and acquisitions. As is the case with virtually every business that merges with or acquires firms that were once competitive, communication, collaboration, and building a unified front can be very challenging, especially in the early days post-merger. One of the greatest and also most elusive promises of a merger between competitive firms is that somehow the combination of different capabilities, cultures, approaches to clients, and so forth will result in a net positive impact on customer relations and on sales. Having worked in an organization many years ago that experienced a spectacular failure after a merger of multi-billion-dollar competitors (i.e., Inacom and Vanstar), I know firsthand that a successful merger is not an inevitable outcome. Leaders have to consider the predictable communication, collaboration, and trust issues that come when competitive firms merge, and that is exactly where my next story about Ken Napolitano begins.

When WheelsUp acquired a competitor recently, Ken immediately began to consider not only things like his new organization's future growth path—where opportunities would arise, and how to pursue them—but he also thought about sensitivities that might exist in the newly merged organization.

"I have to think about where there might be friction," Ken said. "For instance, how do we stay focused on the customer in a time when we're merging two very different cultures? How do we best solve for issues like overlap—overlap in territories, in offerings, in roles? How do we ensure that both sides of the newly integrated sales force are fully engaged?"

The friction Ken referred to comes from overlap issues, and it can also come from disparity in compensation and different cultural expectations and rules. The challenge for the sales leader of an acquiring firm is how to make the acquired team feel a part of the new organization. Ken described some of the differences between the two organizations in a simple and artful way, using the example of how something as simple as the "out of office" reply was viewed differently in the two firms.

"At WheelsUp, it is generally frowned upon to use *out of office* replies because we want our customers to know that we are always available to them," he said. "That is part of WheelsUp's promise to customers and receiving an out of office reply delivers a potentially conflicting message. "But in the group we've acquired, they use *out of office* replies as a common practice."

These are two very different cultures, and Ken and his sales management team need to be respectful of both cultures while also pushing for results. This is a delicate balance to strike, as the expectations that a manager from WheelsUp sets for a salesperson from the acquired firm are going to be different and potentially a source of friction.

The name of the game for Ken and his team, as Ken put it, is to, "Build goodwill in the interest of maximizing revenue." From his standpoint, Ken's three main responsibilities as CSO are the following:

- Maximize revenue
- Promote company / strategic initiatives
- Develop career paths for people

Building goodwill is not simply the right thing to do, but it serves an important purpose, supporting Ken's ability, in this example, to address all three of his main job responsibilities. Perhaps you recognize some of your responsibilities in Ken's list of three. They look very similar to what my responsibilities have been in chief sales/head of sales roles, so they certainly resonate with me.

How does a sales leader build goodwill in the service of the three big objectives above? Ken offers a few ideas.

1. **Cross-pollination.** In the WheelsUp example, Ken is finding ways to bring people from one side of the organization to the other. For example, he may be taking someone from the Business-to-Business (B2B) team to the Business-to-Consumer (B2C) team, giving them new responsibility, and literally integrating them into a new part of the business. Then, by providing support in the form of coaching, development, and maintaining an ongoing interest in this person's career development, he sends a powerful message to the entire organization: "We care about you. We care about your success."

2. **Establishing a common vision of success.** At WheelsUp, although the two merging organizations had different focuses prior to the merger (i.e., B2C versus B2B sales), they now share a common goal and a common customer. As my friend Ed Wallace has written about in his fantastic book, Business Relationships That Last, identifying common goals, passions, and struggles (or as Ed calls it, **"Relational GPS"**) is the key to strong relationships. That is as true for relationships with colleagues as it is for relationships

with customers. In addition to sharing and clarifying that common vision of success for all sellers in his organization, Ken Napolitano is creating the sort of environment in which sellers from both parts of the newly merged organization feel a sense of responsibility for achieving that common vision of success.

3. **Goodwill begets trust.** Trust is a critical component in any sales organization, but it is an especially important part of how we can bring together different people with different perspectives to work together effectively. Important initiatives like cross-selling depend upon sellers trusting one another, sharing information, and having the customer's and the organization's best interests front of mind. They have to trust that the information they share with new colleagues will result in a positive outcome for everyone involved, including themselves. Ken recognizes this, and he knows that demonstrating goodwill, and showing members of his team that he is interested in helping them achieve what they set out to achieve, builds trust. Later in this book, I will talk about the virtuous circle that sales leaders initiate when choosing to make the virtues a driving force in how they lead. This cycle of goodwill begetting trust, trust adding to the goodwill, and so forth in Ken's organization is a concrete example of a virtuous circle.

The story I've shared about Ken highlights goodwill as a practical virtue that is critical to the establishment of an effective post-merger sales organization or to any organization that intends to pursue a cross-selling initiative, but building goodwill clearly has a positive effect in a number of other ways. The impact of an increasing measure of goodwill within a sales organization tends to have direct impact on things like sales staff retention, morale, and motivation, and indirect impact on customer relationships, partners, and an organization's reputation.

Gratitude is very closely related to goodwill. As Tamara Lechner, a self-labeled happiness expert and contributor on Deepak Chopra's blog "Chopra" puts it, "In short, gratitude involves a warm sense of appreciation for somebody or something—it's a sense of goodwill that you can feel in your heart."

Lechner also writes, "Gratitude is both a fleeting emotion and a stable trait—you can be a grateful person or experience a thankful moment. And gratitude can be cultivated."

"There are obstacles that can limit your feelings and expressions of gratitude, such as comparing yourself to others, being lost in the past or overly focused on the future, and getting caught up in a fear of being mocked or being seen as inauthentic."

In Lechner's words, I see a sort of blueprint for engendering gratitude in a sales organization. That blueprint follows:

1. Do what you can as a leader to cultivate a culture of gratitude.
   a. Help your people to see what a privilege it is to serve others. There are myriad ways to do this within your organization, outside of your organization, and in partnership with your customers. Go, and serve others.

2. Don't create the sort of environment where people are constantly comparing themselves to one another. Healthy competition is just that, and it is easy to cross over the line into unhealthy competition.
   a. How do things like competitive rankings fit? Can you balance the need to have a competitive environment with competitive people in it with the need to avoid unnecessary comparisons between people with different capabilities?

3. Learn from the past, but don't dwell on it.

4. Don't focus so much on the future that you neglect the present.

5. Don't make people feel mocked or belittled.

   a. Don't make your sellers feel like public enemy number one when they fail. I've worked in, and consulted with, organizations in which salespeople are belittled behind closed doors or openly treated with disdain by "leaders" who are upset about a seller's performance. Don't expect salespeople to stick around for very long if you have that sort of environment, especially the very talented ones. As they say, talent has a choice.

In the introduction, I categorized goodwill as one of the "other-oriented" virtues, meaning that this virtue manifests itself primarily in the way you treat others. The great saint and theologian Thomas Aquinas tells us that willing and choosing the good of the other is the definition of love. He also tells us that love—the willing the good of the other—is a choice. Even in the most challenging work environments, choosing to demonstrate goodwill—choosing to love, to be abundantly clear—goes a long way. All of us are wired for love. We want others to will our good. Being the recipient of someone else's goodwill begets gratitude, and thus begins a virtuous circle.

I think about my experience working in highly productive sales organizations, and the presence of gratitude and goodwill are one of the key differences between those organizations that were able to sustain success over the course of many years and those organizations that were not. As a seller and as a sales leader, I know what it feels like to work in an environment where gratitude and goodwill are pervasive. What are the ways in which you can engender goodwill and gratitude in your organization and in your daily work as a leader?

Start, Stop, Continue exercise

What can I do right now to build goodwill with my sellers? With clients? With partners? With my colleagues?
What must I stop doing to help eliminate enviousness or forms of ingratitude in my business?
What should I continue doing to build goodwill and a spirit of gratitude within my team? As I work with clients? As I work with partners? As I collaborate with colleagues?

"Patience is the companion of wisdom."

—*St. Augustine*

Chapter Three

The Irate Leader and the Abused Sales Team

Selling is a discipline that requires passion, emotion, and intensity. I'm reminded of my first sales manager, Mike, who knew that he needed to tap into the passions and emotions of his very young, mostly male sales team back in the early '90s. He used to repeat the same five words over and over again until they were drilled into our young sales minds: "Excitement. Enthusiasm. Intensity. Sincerity. Conviction."

That was nearly thirty years ago, and I remember the words and also the feeling that Mike wanted to convey. He knew that he had to tap into our excitement, enthusiasm, etc. to ensure we were ready each day to make one hundred calls per day and hit our sales targets. When he thought it necessary, Mike would demonstrate excitement or intensity or whichever characteristic he thought the team was lacking in the moment. For all of his positive energy, Mike also had moments where we weren't meeting expectations as a team, and he let us have it.

It wasn't unusual for him to round up the team in the main conference room and to holler at us at the top of his lungs. These were not fun meetings, and Mike was pretty intense. He is also physically imposing, and while I know he wouldn't have gotten physical with anyone on the team, the environment was charged enough to feel like a fight could break out at any moment.

I'm not going to beat Mike up for doing what he did. In fact, I empathize with him to an extent based on the ragtag team he was dealing with and how undisciplined we really were. Most of us were in our mid-twenties, and we didn't have a clue what we were doing. It must have been frustrating to lead a team like that, and for the most part, Mike kept his negative emotions in check.

Not all sales leaders do, unfortunately. One of the most damaging things a sales manager can do is to let his or her anger over a performance issue become the focal point instead of the performance issue itself. I don't mean the chair-throwing, expletive-laden, I-need-anger-management-training kind of anger. That would be totally unprofessional and not acceptable. I am talking about when frustration over a performance issue causes a sales manager to lose focus and pursue a less-than-productive resolution to the problem at hand.

Keeping Anger In Check

In my work as a sales leadership coach and advisor, I work one-on-one with CSOs, VPs, and directors, down to frontline sales managers. I'm reminded of a young sales leader who worked for a specialty medical device company a few years ago. I was struck by how junior he was when we first met, but I was impressed with his career accomplishments and the rapid trajectory he was on in a hot market space. He was very smart, personable, and upon first meeting, I could tell why senior leaders put their trust in him to run the sales team despite his relative lack of sales leadership experience. He was convincing, and he seemed very confident.

This hotshot sales leader was tasked with growing sales in a recently merged organization, and he was asked to do so while merging sales cultures, sales operating systems and data, sales territories and teams, comp plans, and so forth. His former organization (one of the two being merged) had a relatively complex sale that took time to execute. The other sales organization had a less complex sale and a shorter sales cycle. As it turned out, the more this young sales leader investigated and understood the reality within his newly merged organization, the more concerned he became about the new organization's ability to fully integrate and generate the 1+1=3 sort of result that drove the merger in the first place.

Over the course of two to three months, I saw a very enthusiastic, lighthearted young leader degenerate into a dark, discouraged, at times nasty leader. As a coach and advisor, I had to bear with him, as I understood the pressure he felt. As a salesperson and as a fellow sales leader, however, I found his approach to the job over time to be demotivating for those around him.

He demonstrated that he could not control his frustrations or his anger. His judgment appeared clouded. Rather than seeing the way forward or the way out of the mess he had been handed, he chose to (mis)direct his anger toward the people he needed most to be successful. His salespeople were frequently the targets of tirades that were aimed at individuals or whole teams, and those tirades usually stemmed from someone not meeting an expectation, e.g., not filling out a call report or missing a detail on a forecast report, especially an expectation that this sales leader felt had been clearly articulated.

There was a sort of self-indulgence to the way he approached mistakes and performance problems among sellers. He would bemoan poor performance publicly by saying things like, "What part of 'fill out a call plan' wasn't clear? Is it me, or is that really simple to understand?" I'm paraphrasing, but you get the gist. When he saw examples of poor performance, his reactions tended to sound like, "Why are they (i.e., his salespeople) doing this to me?" In his anger and self-indulgence, he missed two of the most likely reasons why people weren't meeting performance expectations:

1. They didn't understand the expectations that were set for them.

2. They weren't equipped or able to meet those expectations.

And while salespeople bear some responsibility if they don't understand expectations or don't know how to meet them, it is ultimately the leader's responsibility to solve those problems. This particular leader chose to indulge in anger and frustration, and he did it so much that he lost the support of the sales organization. In a matter of months, he also lost the support of the same executive team that had vaulted him into a position of great responsibility at a relatively early age. They didn't trust his ability to keep his anger in check, and ultimately, they didn't trust him to solve the problem of unclear expectations and developing the team to meet expectations going forward.

What is a sales leader to do when faced with the (at times) extremely frustrating situations that we have to confront? My first bit of perhaps obvious advice is to avoid acting like the last leader I described.

While it can be incredibly difficult to keep your frustration in check when you're in the pivotal and most challenging role, the best-performing sales leaders choose to do exactly that. As is the case with most challenging situations, you know intuitively that approaching challenges with a sense of calm and with patience is almost always the better path compared to allowing frustration to take hold. I have a story and some principles to share that will help you put patience and calmness into practice as a sales leader . . . even on your most frustrating days.

The Brain Battle

Before we go there, I found some interesting information that explains some of the brain physiology behind when we feel angry. Did you know that there is an almond-shaped part of the brain that is associated with emotions? It's called the amygdala, and it is activated when we are confronted by things that make us feel anxious, afraid, or angry.

In a recent *Harvard Medicine* magazine article titled, "Anger Management," Elizabeth Dougherty describes a study led by Darin Dougherty, an associate professor of psychiatry at Massachusetts General Hospital.

"During angry recollections, the amygdala fired. At the same time, a part of the orbital frontal cortex, just above the eyes, also engaged, putting the brakes on emotion. 'Healthy people experience anger,' says [Darin] Dougherty, 'but they can suppress it before acting on it.'"

If you have ever felt like there was a battle going on in your head when you're extremely frustrated or angry, that is because there really is a battle under way between the amygdala and the orbital frontal cortex.

I found a fascinating article in the Harvard Business Review, written by Diane Musho Hamilton, an internationally recognized mediator and the author of *Everything is Workable: A Zen Approach to Conflict Resolution*. In the article, Hamilton writes:

When we perceive a threat, the amygdala sounds an alarm,

releasing a cascade of chemicals in the body. Stress hormones like adrenaline and cortisol flood our system, immediately preparing us for fight or flight. When this deeply instinctive function takes over, we call it what Daniel Goleman coined in Emotional Intelligence as "amygdala hijack." In common psychological parlance we say, "We've been triggered." We notice immediate changes like an increased heart rate or sweaty palms. Our breathing becomes more shallow and rapid as we take in more oxygen, preparing to bolt if we have to.

The flood of stress hormones create other sensations like a quivering in our solar plexus, limbs, or our voice. We may notice heat flush our face, our throat constrict, or the back of our neck tighten and jaw set. We are in the grip of a highly efficient, but prehistoric set of physiological responses. These sensations are not exactly pleasant—they're not meant for relaxation. They're designed to move us to action.

The active amygdala also immediately shuts down the neural pathway to our prefrontal cortex so we can become disoriented in a heated conversation. Complex decision-making disappears, as does our access to multiple perspectives. As our attention narrows, we find ourselves trapped in the one perspective that makes us feel the most safe: "I'm right and you're wrong," even though we ordinarily see more perspectives.

And if that wasn't enough, our memory becomes untrustworthy. Have you ever been in a fight with your partner or friend, and you literally can't remember a positive thing about them? It's as though the brain drops the memory function altogether in an effort to survive the threat. When our memory is compromised like this, we can't recall something from the past that might help us calm down. In fact, we can't remember much of anything. Instead, we're simply filled with the flashing red light of the amygdala indicating "Danger, react. Danger, protect. Danger, attack."

In the throes of amygdala hijack, we can't choose how we want to react because the old protective mechanism in the nervous system does it for us—even before we glimpse that there could be a choice. It is ridiculous.

It seems this inner battle between the amygdala and the orbital frontal cortex is not something we can easily control or tamp down once it begins. There are ways, however, for us to cope while this battle is going on in our brains.

I did some research on ways that we can effectively "exercise" the orbital frontal cortex to make sure it can put the brakes on the amygdala. Not surprisingly, mental exercises such as meditation, deep breathing, and prayer are recommended, so therein lies the prescription: Go work out that orbital frontal cortex. I will wait here while you pray or meditate, and then I will share an inspiring story about how calmness and patience manifested themselves in a highly successful team's development.

The Value of Patience

Mareo McCracken is a wildly successful seller and sales leader. Currently the chief customer officer at Movemedical, his selling and leadership career spans the software, automotive, commodities, investment management, transportation, and medical device industries. He has nearly 40,000 followers on LinkedIn, and he has been a contributor for *Inc. Magazine* and Thrive Global's blog. He also just published his first book, *Really Care For Them*, about the power of showing people you care to build trust and increase sales. I spoke with Mareo recently about an experience that he had early in his sales career, and this experience taught him the value of patience in leading sales teams.

In Mareo's first sales job, he worked on a team that traveled together frequently, working in a new hotel or city practically every day. They were business consultants to small business owners who wanted to build a website or market online for the first time. The team Mareo served on would run seminars with a few hundred people, and they would sell attendees internet marketing packages to help them get their businesses online.

"Our team comprised seven to ten salespeople and one sales manager," Mareo explained. "We were like a sports team. We traveled everywhere together, we would share rooms, meals, etc. My manager was very competitive and very aggressive . . . almost to the point of abusive. Most of us were former athletes, and we were used to receiving pretty direct feedback. Not always coaching, but we definitely received feedback. For the most part, we let the negativity roll off us.

"We had team meetings two or three times per day, and we would have huddle sessions with our manager. There were many times when you didn't know what to do next because you were so focused on not messing things up. You were so worried about not getting in trouble that you weren't really thinking about selling. One of the reasons there was so much pressure to simply not mess up was the team's compensation structure. The whole team got paid based on aggregate performance."

No matter how many sales they personally brought in, they were paid a commission rate based on the aggregate average of all team members' sales. This caused a lot of competition within the team, and it also caused Mareo's manager to be very aggressive in his behavior toward the team.

The company's sales force was roughly one hundred people, and the team Mareo was part of comprised people who were stars or were at least perceived as star players. They were like an all-star team—smart, highly capable, and hard-working. "We all wanted to be the top team, to be the best team in the country," he said, "and yet, there were other sales teams who were getting better results than we were."

Mareo and his teammates wanted to know why, so they asked their manager if they could go out and visit with these other teams to see what they were doing differently. "It was sort of like a spy mission for us. We wanted to know what they were doing that was getting better results, and our manager approved us going out to infiltrate and observe these teams. We went out on one of our weeks off (when we weren't traveling to seminars as a team ourselves), and we observed what these teams were doing differently. When we came back, three of us had exactly the same feedback based on what we observed about the other teams."

Their team culture was different, and their managers' behavior was different. "Their managers didn't make them feel badly when they made mistakes. The higher-performing teams focused on discussing what went wrong and finding a way to make sure that it didn't happen again. It was always about *what can we do better*, and their managers demonstrated patience."

It really was a lesson in patience, as their managers calmly accepted when things didn't go the right way. Examples of statements that Mareo and his colleagues heard when observing the other team included: "We didn't get this deal. What did we learn that we can apply to winning the next five deals?"

"That was entirely different from the way our team handled losses," Mario said. "We got plenty of feedback, but we rarely talked about the important lessons we learned and how we could approach the situation better next time."

Before giving this feedback to their manager, Mareo and his colleagues were all certain they were going to get in trouble.

When they told him about what they observed of the other teams, however, his reaction was surprising and very positive. He accepted the feedback, and to his credit, he listened.

"He shared with us that he thought the best way to motivate his team was to put fear of failure center stage to ensure we wanted to work as hard as he wanted us to work," Mareo said. "In the end, our motivation level as a team had nothing to do with hard work, but it had everything to do with our emotional state when engaging with clients. When we approached our work from this place of fear and pressure, we weren't really thinking about our clients. We were too busy worrying about ourselves and whether we were going to get in trouble to focus in an appropriate way on our clients' needs." In this way, the environment and the team culture that Mareo's manager created had become a barrier to his team's success and also to their clients' success.

"We were never the low-price provider," Mario said, "so we had to sell our services based on value. Also, given the fact that our customers were small to mid-size business (SMB) owners, they typically had difficulty getting access to credit. We needed to help clients find creative ways to pay for the solutions we sold. This situation got much worse when the credit crunch began at the end of 2007. Because we were able to focus more deeply on our client's needs, we were better able to address credit challenges for them. That enabled us to win and to continue to perform at a high level, even when the credit environment took a bad turn."

There is also a lesson in humility here. The way Mareo's manager led his team prior to the feedback team members gave was all learned behavior. He showed great humility and vulnerability when receiving their feedback, and that made it possible for him to receive his team's feedback and act upon it immediately. He didn't let his ego get in the way. It took time for him to change and become a really effective manager, but he kept working at it.

"Our manager's more patient approach enabled us to focus on our clients more deeply," Mareo said. "Our accountability stemmed no longer from our sales manager, but we were now accountable to our clients . . . and getting them results, and that led directly to our being more effective at winning more business.

"An indirect result of our manager changing his approach was that our team really started functioning like a team. We helped one another. We cared about each other's development, and we even coached one another when the opportunity presented itself."

All salesperson's statistics were reported daily, and whether they were first or worst, their name and their performance were shown on this report. "We called it the 'BCS Report' after the college football Bowl Championship Series rankings, which was a new thing in the college sports world at the time. This kind of ranking had the potential to be problematic because of the impact it could have on morale. The way that our team looked at it was not so much about whether any members of our team made the top of the 'BCS Report' as a top performer, but instead, we cared more about how many members of our team made it to the top or near the top of the list. That was more important to us. We would rather have had all ten of our teammates appear on the top-twenty list than have one or two of our people make the top of the list.

"We became the top-performing sales team for the next six months, until the organization broke up our team and distributed us out into different teams, presumably to help pollenate other teams with the way we did our jobs. The team's sales results increased by 30 percent in that period, and it was largely due to the shift in our team's culture and our manager's choice to take a more patient approach with us.

"In 2008, the company's business model changed, and my sales manager left. He went on to become a VP of sales at three tech companies, and he has had great success in those roles."

What does Mareo's story teach us?

First, demonstrating impatience, frustration, and anger can impact relationships between a leader and his or her team in a negative way. In this case, Mareo's manager learned earlier in his career that things like fear—fear of failure and fear of some managers themselves—were proper motivators. In reality, they were the opposite. Demonstrating anger and impatience when sellers didn't meet behavioral expectations did not help in this case. In my many years as a seller and sales leader, I can't think of a single example where anger and impatience helped to strengthen relationships within a sales team or serve to properly motivate people.

Angry, impatient managers are generally unable to tap into the intrinsic motivations of sellers, as they typically don't take the time to identify and understand the intrinsic motivators of each member of the team in the first place. When you are impatient for results, you don't make time to understand these personal, deep-seated motivators. As a result, impatient managers have to rely strictly on extrinsic means to motivate and encourage the right behavior among their sellers.

I read an article on the Healthline website recently, "What Is Extrinsic Motivation, And Is It Effective?" by A. Rochaun Meadows-Fernandez. In the article, Meadows-Fernandez writes, "A major drawback to using extrinsic motivation is knowing what to do when the reward is gone or its value is exhausted. There's also the possibility of dependency on the reward. The usefulness of extrinsic motivators should be evaluated on a case-by-case and person-by-person basis."

A key takeaway from that article is that extrinsic motivators are finite and can create a sort of unhealthy dependence among those who use them to motivate others. Putting this in the context of the relationship between a sales leader and a seller, if all that I have at my disposal to motivate is extrinsic motivators (i.e., rewards and consequences), then I don't really have a way to impact a seller's motivation when rewards are less valuable or consequences are less relevant. However, if I am patient enough to invest in understanding each team member's intrinsic motivators and to take a patient approach to giving feedback and coaching, then I am far more likely to successfully encourage the right behavior among my team. A patient leader takes the time to properly diagnose all that needs to be understood about his or her environment—about clients, about opportunities, about competitors, and perhaps most important, about the sellers who do the work of differentiating and winning every day. A deeper understanding of sellers' intrinsic motivators as well as how sellers' behavior might need to change to bring about desired results is crucial for sales leaders who want sustainable success. This requires taking a patient approach.

Patience is one of the "self-oriented" virtues because it causes us to slow down and evaluate which behavior is most important and most effective for the situation at hand. This virtue helps us to put the proverbial brakes on our emotions and on our thought process to bring about better thinking and hopefully, a better outcome.

As you move into the next Start, Stop, Continue exercise, consider if and how you can train yourself to be better at managing your anger in those weaker moments (that you will inevitably have). How can you maintain a calm demeanor in the face of frustration? How can you maintain an appropriate amount of patience in trying situations?

Start, Stop, Continue exercise

What can I do right now to demonstrate an appropriate degree of patience and/or calmness with my sellers? With clients? With partners? With my colleagues?

What must I/we stop doing to prevent bursts of anger or impatience from damaging our team spirit, motivation, and focus?

What should I continue doing to encourage patience and calm among my teammates? As I work with clients? As I work with partners? As I collaborate with colleagues?

"Diligence is the mother of good fortune, and the goal of a good intention was never reached through its opposite, laziness."

—*Miguel de Cervantes*

"Diligence and hard work sensitize you to recognize opportunity."

—*David P. Ingerson*

Chapter Four

The Slothful Sales Manager

We all know the stereotype of the "Desk Jockey" sales manager. He sits behind his desk, looking at reports all day, firing off emails when people don't have their pipeline or forecast data totally accurate. He rarely goes out into the field because . . . well, because. He works sixty or seventy hours a week, often working the wee morning hours or late nights, reading reports, firing off emails and texts, and generally doing a lot.

A sales manager who demonstrates this behavior might not typically be labeled lazy, but I'm going to do it. The busy Desk Jockey is lazy. Before you violently disagree with me, indulge me for a few moments.

Management Stereotypes

There are other sales management types that I would like to call out, as well:

- The Super Heroes: Their days are dominated by saving deals or saving calls. They rarely catch problems with deals until the eleventh hour, but when they see them, they swoop in with their super skills to solve them.

- The Star Players: They don't coach or train anyone. They model. Their people need to watch them operate to understand what great looks like.

- The Big Picture Gals or Guys: Keeping it "big picture" means these managers don't need to worry about the details.

- The Vampires: Unavailable during the day, these managers get work done at night, when no one can respond to their emails.

- The Social Chairs: Having tough conversations is never a priority for these social animals. They devote most of their spare time to organizing happy hours and social events where, sometimes, business gets done.

You may recognize some or all of these sales manager stereotypes among past colleagues or sales organizations. Some of the folks from your past who resemble one or more of these stereotypes might not fit into your traditional definition of lazy, so I will explain.

Each day, a sales manager is faced with issues that range from strategic to tactical, from people issues to compensation, structure, prioritization, reporting, data issues, and the list goes on. While it is important for a sales manager to focus on one important thing at a time, to focus on just one aspect of the job at the exclusion of other important aspects of the job is a form of laziness.

The Desk Jockey must break away from his desk and help/serve his team out in the field. Why? Because the team's development and their manager's coaching are inextricably linked. The Star Player must adapt her approach to her team's development because modeling behavior alone is not enough. Modeling is effective when you want to help sellers be more conscious of where they're falling short and how they can act differently. Modeling isn't sufficient when sellers understand their shortcomings already. That's when they need their sales manager to coach. The Big Picture Guy needs to come back down to earth sometimes and help his people with the details because the details matter. He can't "strategize" his team to a higher state of effectiveness or expect details to take care of themselves.

We sales managers don't have the luxury of being focused on only one thing like our stereotypical managers attempt to do. Every day, we have to be diligent and lively when moving from one priority issue or opportunity to another. There simply is no other way to approach the work of a sales leader.

The Impact of Diligence

When I think of diligence and a lively approach to the work of sales management, I think of my friend Julia Flohr. Julia is a very high achiever in pretty much every aspect of her life . . . as a mother, as an athlete, and as a professional seller and sales leader. She told me a story recently about her experience and her first huge success as a leader at McGraw-Hill Higher Education, and it really resonated with me.

Julia was hired to be a district manager for an underperforming district at McGraw-Hill Higher Ed.

"I was asked to take on a new team that had not been achieving its goals," she said. "One of the people having performance issues had lost $1.5 million in sales. I had to move the lowest performer off the team within the first six weeks."

When she took over, Julia's first-year goal for the team had little to do with the numbers or the money she could earn. "The goal was to build the best team in higher ed sales. If I built the best team, the money would come."

Why was it hard to build the best team? "I was measured by my financial performance, and I knew that was ultimately the way my team and I would be measured. We had a really long way to go. We needed to turn most of the team over. Six out of the nine people were brand new.

"Before my arrival, the team was not held accountable, and the previous manager was not really engaged. I was told by my most senior rep that they were 'on an island.' No one talked to other members of the team, and the team was at absolute rock bottom in every way—performance and morale especially. They needed me to be there with them, actively involved, getting to know every client in the territory. I lived on the road with my team. We lived on campus. I made it my job to be on the road with them."

Julia made a point of celebrating the team's accomplishments. "I came up with something called the 'End of the Road' to celebrate the team's effort at the end of our selling season." Being engaged with this team on a daily basis was what was required.

"I had to document everything," Julia said. "Justify why we needed two additional people on the team, for example, by taking a hard look at the work that each person on the team was doing. Two of my people were stretched beyond capacity, so I needed to jump in and really understand their capacity and what could be done to alleviate some of the burden they bore."

The moral of the story is that a diligent leader balances the need to be laser-focused with the need to shift priorities, to be agile about the work. Only the most diligent managers are able to shift their focus and their most effective effort toward their team's most important needs, even when they frequently change. Sales teams led by a highly diligent leader are inspired to be active but also thoughtful in their approach to the issues and opportunities they face every day.

Going back to Julia's story, the team she inherited did not appear to want to do the work, and their behavior was not what Julia wanted to see. She had to model the sort of diligence that would be required of each member of the team because they did not have a clear sense of what great performance and hard work looked like in this environment. On top of modeling what diligence and hard work looks like for the team, Julia had some tough decisions to make on the talent front.

Julia had a Digital Learning Consultant (DLC) on her team who was very smart and capable but was likely to be more successful in a sales rep role than in her current one. Julia had to have the tough conversation with this DLC about that. It was very difficult for this member of Julia's team, but she took it with grace. That set up a strong partnership between Julia and the former DLC-turned-sales rep. Two years later, she was rep of the year, and the diligence with which she approached her job was a big part of why she was so successful.

This is an example of the impact that a very diligent and active manager can have on a high-potential/low-performance player. This particular consultant could easily have failed in her role, but her commitment and the commitment of her leader and coach to work diligently together at improving every day was the key to her great success.

By year two, Julia's goal was that her team be the number-one team in the country. Julia's team achieved that goal, exceeding its goal by $5.3 million, a significant increase above the prior year's performance. At the company's awards ceremony, Julia's team dominated the stage—six out of the ten highest achievers on the main stage were from her team:

- Newcomer of the Year
- Digital Learning Consultant of the Year
- District Manager of the Year
- Three of the Top Ten Performers in the Country

I asked Julia where her work ethic came from, and she pointed to her family and her upbringing as the source and inspiration.

"My grandfather started a machine shop in Dundalk, Maryland," she said. "He emigrated from Italy, worked from 7 a.m. until 11 p.m. every day. He never stopped. My single mother was the same way. Living with my grandparents and my mother as my example engrained in me the very hard work ethic that I apply to my work.

"I was once told, 'You're never going to manage [someone like] yourself,' meaning I shouldn't expect people on my team to be just like me. I'd be setting them up for failure by setting unrealistic expectations.

"But I can set clear expectations for my team. You're going to work hard, but you're going to have fun. You're going to put in the work, but you're going to have a good time doing it. That's what I expect, and if they're not having fun, we have to fix that."

Another example of how diligence plays out in a sales leader's work can be found in a story I heard from Ryan Ward. Ryan is currently the area vice president of sales at iRhythm Technologies, but when I first met him, he was an area vice president (AVP) at Medtronic Advanced Energy. His example is one of diligence in the area of expectation setting, communication, and alignment.

Ryan was given the opportunity to be head of sales for MDT Advanced Energy, a well-deserved promotion that came for two reasons. First, he was recognized as a high-potential leader who had demonstrated great effectiveness in his role as an AVP.

Second, the business needed a new head of sales, as the general manager (GM) and the VP of sales had both decided to leave the organization within a month of one another. Both the GM and the VP of sales were deeply connected to the sales organization, so Ryan had to step in and immediately demonstrate that he could fill a big void.

"There was a lot of concern when the GM and VP left because they were so deeply involved with the sales organization. A lot of people were concerned. Their *Spidey senses* were raised because of the GM and the VP's departure," Ryan explained.

Internally, from a corporate standpoint, there seemed to be some undue frustration with the Advanced Energy business unit's ability to hit top-line objectives. "When I came into the new role, having been promoted in an untraditional way by an outgoing GM, it was a strange way to start out in the role that I always wanted to play. On top of that, I had a brand-new GM who came from a different part of MDT's business, and so there was a sort of learning curve for both of us." The new GM needed to get acclimated to Ryan's business unit, and Ryan needed to quickly demonstrate he could solve the business problems that the business faced at the time.

"I was being judged based on my ability to meet expectations, right out of the gate."

Ryan's initial goal was to stabilize the sales channel and to give the salespeople confidence in the organization's direction and what they were trying to achieve. "I had to get the organization aligned to achieve the result we could deliver," he said. They re-established quotas, and they also reset the compensation structure and model. "Quota and compensation alignment would be critical to breathe some new life and health into my existing sales team."

Overall, the business's goal and therefore Ryan's goal was to deliver on their committed sales target. Ryan recalls a conversation he had with the VP of finance, in which they established an ongoing dialogue about what the business could deliver. "There was a misalignment between what corporate thought we could deliver versus what we could actually deliver. We needed to get aligned on the corporate target number versus what we had a real chance to deliver." Ryan worked diligently with the finance VP to establish a stretch goal for the Advanced Energy business that corporate leadership would support and that the people in his business unit would see as attainable.

The diligence that Ryan applied to expectation setting, communicating up and down the command chain, and to driving alignment of quota and incentives with the business's overarching goals was the biggest driver for his success in the role. Another key driver was Ryan's ongoing commitment to the coaching and development of his staff of sales managers. He has been a champion of coaching throughout his tenure as a sales leader.

"We hit our top-line, and we absolutely crushed our bottom-line goals," Ryan said. He did so while focusing heavily on managing budgets, changing staffing levels and account management structure, and tightening expenses. He did all of this while trying to minimize disruption to the sales effort.

What conclusions can we come to based on Julia's and Ryan's examples of diligence?

First, regardless of the specific needs of the business and its sales organization, diligence is a critical attribute for sales leaders. Note that I didn't say "hard work" is a critical attribute. That is a given. Merriam-Webster's definition of diligence follows:

Diligence (a): steady, earnest, and energetic effort: devoted and painstaking work and application to accomplish an undertaking

Julia Flohr and Ryan Ward offer us examples of diligence at work in two very different situations. It was not simply their willingness to put in extra hours that led to their success, but it was their steady, earnest, and energetic effort toward the right things that led to it. Their focus, their "devoted and painstaking work," and their dogged pursuit of the specific objective they had to achieve at McGraw-Hill and Medtronic, respectively, is why there were so successful.

Steady, Earnest, Energetic

What does it mean to be steady, earnest, and energetic in your work? Steadiness implies a certain predictability and stick-to-itiveness in the way a person goes about a task. This is particularly difficult for a sales leader because of the dynamic nature of the job. And yet, the best sales leaders find a way to achieve that predictability, that steadiness that gives their teams confidence and an example to follow.

If I observed you over the course of a quarter or over a year, would I witness a predictable, steady, dogged approach to how you pursue your objectives? Or would I witness someone who allows herself or himself to be diverted, or someone who is not-so-steady in their approach?

What about the energy level or the earnestness with which you approach the most important parts of your job? Do you attack critical parts of the work like coaching and development, alignment, clear communication and expectation setting, or whatever is most critical to your current role, or do you only get to those things when you can?

Diligent sales leaders are ones who demonstrate to their team, and to their peers and colleagues up and across the organizational chart, that they are working hard at the right things. I've known leaders who work sixteen-hour days who I do not consider to be particularly diligent. Some leaders work hard at the wrong things. In doing so, they inadvertently set a terrible example for their teams. Putting a twist on the old adage, "Work smarter, not harder." I would like to offer this simple alternative: ***Work diligently.***

I categorized diligence as one of the "self-oriented" virtues because it helps us to govern our own effort and energy. Diligence helps us to fully and steadily apply our brain power and our personal resources to achieve whatever outcome we seek to achieve.

What is it that your business or your team needs right now that requires your steady, earnest, and most energetic effort? Go to the Start, Stop, Continue exercise, and capture your ideas for how to make a more diligent effort right now.

Start, Stop, Continue exercise

What can I do right now to demonstrate diligence with my sellers? With clients? With partners? With my colleagues?
What must I stop doing to avoid giving the impression that I am not working hard at critical tasks or at the right things?
What should I continue doing to model diligence for my team? As I work with clients? As I work with partners? As I collaborate with colleagues?

"Generosity is the most natural outward expression of an inner attitude of compassion and loving-kindness."

—*Dalai Lama*

"Joy is a sign of generosity. When you are full of joy, you move faster, and you want to go about doing good to everyone."

—*Mother Teresa*

Chapter Five

Avarice and the Love of Money Is the Root of All Evil

Money isn't the root of all evil, but the *love of money*, also called cupidity, is. Some in their desire for money stray so far from what is right and good that they end up inflicting great pain on themselves, on their teams, and on their customers.

Winning At All Costs

Early in my sales career, I came to know a sales manager, we'll call him Evan to protect his real identity, whose love of money and the trappings of success were the single greatest driving force behind his work. When I first met him, he seemed like a very personable, positive, and happy person. He was quick with a joke, and he had a great sense of humor. He was a really likeable guy.

Evan and I worked for the same company for a few years, and on the sales floor, he would frequently boast about his income, the latest all-inclusive Caribbean vacation he went on, how much money he spent on extravagant meals, booze, and gambling. I was young, so it all sounded very exciting, and to be honest, the lifestyle he described was really appealing to me. I come from a middle-class family, and we didn't go on many vacations. We certainly didn't go on extravagant, all-inclusive trips, so the world he described sounded exciting to me.

Over time, though, I witnessed a different side of him. His drive for more money, more trips, more of everything took the shape of a *win at all costs* mentality. He often looked past—or worse, encouraged—unethical behavior by members of his team because, in his mind, the end justified the means.

As a leader, Evan demonstrated behavior that was really detrimental to the development of the salespeople he hired. They learned that putting the end goal of earning money ahead of doing things the right way was not only acceptable but encouraged. Principles like putting customers first were not taught. In fact, the environment this manager created made a mockery of the principle of customer focus. It was all about him and the salespeople who needed to earn. They loved money, and they didn't love their customers.

You can probably guess how things turned out for Evan. Eventually, he lost the trust of his customers, which led to the loss of trust by his team and the president of the company. He was let go for yet another transgression that he tried to justify based on his need to earn. I learned a few years later that he carried the same cupidity into his next role, which also ended badly. He was a very talented and likeable person who allowed his love of money and the rich rewards of sales success to blind him.

Distorting the Culture

Cupidity and greed can also infect entire leadership teams. Malcolm Simmonds, the food service industry executive I spoke of earlier, told me a story about a company he was intimately familiar with that illustrates this perfectly.

A private equity firm was running the company. After the family that founded the company lost control, a management firm was brought in to run day-to-day operations. Malcolm witnessed a level of greed so rampant that it distorted the culture. He pointed to the incentive compensation plan as an example. "Executive team member's incentive plans were in the millions versus employees' remuneration if they could get the profit up," he said. "That drove bad, short-term decision making."

The executive team pushed changes that would have increased profits at the expense of employees and customers. While that was going on, Malcolm said, "the company decided to relocate to a nicer HQ office building . . . with an executive wing that had security and pass card protection. The general workforce called it affectionately 'green mile,' alluding to the high-paid team."

You may recall the film *The Green Mile* was about a prison, specifically the death row inmates and guards who occupied an exclusive stretch of the jail. In a way, the executive team that Malcolm describes not only set themselves apart and against the interests of the people they led, but they created a sort of prison for themselves. It was similar to the proverbial prison that Evan created for himself.

In both examples, greed and cupidity led to leaders who were ultimately not trusted by their teams or by their customers. They ended up isolated from the people who they were supposed to serve, and it was all for the love of money and the trappings of success.

These are real and somewhat extreme examples of how greed and the love of money above all things can cause us to operate in ways that are anathema to effective sales leadership. Because you are reading this book, I will not dwell on what you already recognize as unacceptable behavior. The issue I need to remind you of is that each of us may be tempted to act like Evan, on occasion. In fact, Evan wasn't all bad. He had a kind heart and a great sense of humor. On occasion, he was very generous. He just had frequent ethical lapses that he justified because there was money to be made. Unfortunately, those lapses caused him to lose friends on a personal and on a business level.

Generosity Pays Off

If greed and the behavior it causes are undesirable in life and in sales leadership, then we should take a hard look at how its opposing virtue, generosity, can positively affect our work and our relationships with our teams. Generosity comes in more than just one form. Being generous with rewards, money, or gifts is relevant to the job of a sales leader, but being generous with our time, our support, or our own resources, strengths, and capabilities is just as relevant.

In my own experience, generosity has played a huge role in building teams that were highly motivated and put in their best effort. Aside from the rewards I have ensured people receive for doing great work, for going above and beyond, I have also made a point of being generous with my time. In addition to the recurring blocks of time that I tend to spend with members of my team, I also make a point of being highly responsive, offering my time at all hours when necessary, to help a teammate.

I learned this lesson the hard way, as I was once on the receiving end of a less-than-generous leader's treatment. She was stingy with her time and with her support, and despite my strong results and consistently high level of effort, there were times when she was unresponsive. I recall how she treated other members of the team, and to a person, everyone concluded that she simply didn't care enough to give us her time. I decided back then that I would be as responsive as I could possibly be to the members of my team, and I would never make them feel unimportant by holding back my time, my energy, or my resources. A generous leader engenders a team environment in which people are willing to share with others.

The best sellers I know are not coin-operated humans who are motivated by money. Every one of them would rather feel a great sense of purpose in their work and be able to achieve something important for their families or for their communities long before they achieve recognition for themselves. The best sales leaders know how to tap into their people's motivation by demonstrating a generous spirit. I will give all that I have to help you succeed, including my most precious asset, my time.

Thinking about you and your team, ask yourself: How can I expect sellers on my team to be generous with their time, their strengths, and their resources if I don't demonstrate my own form of generosity?

Generosity is one of the "other-oriented" virtues because it manifests itself in the giving of something (i.e., our time, our ideas) to others who are in need. We cannot simply be generous to ourselves. Others must receive that generosity for it to be realized.

Ask yourself, what changes can I make in the way I demonstrate generosity to my team? Can I do better? How?

Start, Stop, Continue exercise

What can I do right now to demonstrate generosity with my sellers? With clients? With partners? With my colleagues?
What must I stop doing to avoid over-emphasizing money as the "why" behind my work or my team's work?
What should I continue doing to demonstrate generosity as I work with our clients? As I work with partners? As I collaborate with colleagues?

"Discipline yourself, and others won't need to."

—John Wooden

"The ability to subordinate an impulse to a value is the essence of the proactive person."

—Stephen R. Covey

Chapter Six

Prone to Gluttony

I've observed sales leaders over the years whose behavior indicates that they feel entitled to be *excessively indulgent* in front of their customers and their teams. Synonyms for *excessively indulgent* include piggish, rapacious, grasping, covetous, insatiable, predatory, voracious, and grabby. None of those are admirable labels for people in sales or leadership roles. I know I would be insulted if someone were to hang one of those labels on me.

The Excessive Winer

To illustrate what excessive indulgence can look like in a professional selling environment, I will offer a quick story. I once worked with a sales leader who was incredibly skilled as a seller, and by all accounts, he was successful in several high-profile sales roles in the tech and consulting industries. He was intellectually brilliant, and he was a very effective coach, particularly in major, complex sales scenarios. We were out to dinner with a client of ours, and the client had hired us in the year prior for a major project. We met earlier that afternoon to hammer out the details of another major project to follow on to the first very successful project. The dinner we had scheduled was both a gesture of thanks to our major client, and also an opportunity to strengthen some of the personal bonds between the senior-most executives from both companies.

We chose to meet at an expensive and very highly rated restaurant. Everyone, from the senior executives to our client, was looking forward to the meal. Our server came to the table to take drink orders. The sales leader asked a few questions, pressing the server for details about wines that she clearly did not know. He did so ostensibly to show everyone at the table how much he knew about wine. There might have been a few eye rolls at the table, and a couple of those eyeballs rolling might have been mine. When the server couldn't answer some of the sales leader's questions, the leader became impatient and asked for the sommelier. More eyes rolled, not because of the request to see the sommelier but because of the self-importance with which the request was made. I believe the words were, "I demand to see the sommelier."

Several of us at the table, client included, were mortified.

The sommelier came. Questions were answered, and expensive bottles of wine were ordered. The key moment came after everyone had ordered and eaten and, despite nearly everyone at the table feeling full, the sales leader insisted on ordering his favorite and most obscenely expensive wine for the dessert course. Had he bothered to read the expressions at the table, he would have recognized that no one wanted another bite or sip, and some of us, the client included, were starting to feel uncomfortable about the sheer excess of it all. Our clients were a tightly run, by-the-book kind of operation, and I could tell they were getting uncomfortable with what was becoming a remarkably expensive dinner.

Several days after the dinner, I was told in no uncertain terms that this client didn't really enjoy the company of that sales leader. I received a loud and clear message that they would only deal with me and would prefer not to deal with my sales leader. They didn't go into much detail, but it was clear that the sales leader had missed the chance to connect with them. His excessive indulgence in front of the client left a bad taste in their mouths. He had blown our opportunity to deepen and extend our relationship with the client that night, and it was all because of his piggish, self-oriented actions.

There is no more effective way to send the message, "I'm going to take care of myself first," than to indulge your own desires in an extravagant way in front of those you serve—especially your team and your customers.

Excessive indulgence is not a good look for anyone, but for those of us in sales leadership roles, it is especially damaging to our reputations and relationships. We salespeople already have a reputation for being too money-motivated, too mercenary, and we practically have to dig ourselves out of a hole before we ever say a word when we make a sales call to a new contact. We must do what we can to change the perception of our profession, and that change starts with sales leaders.

Mastering Self-Control

What can we do to avoid being tagged as excessively indulgent? We can get a hold of ourselves! We can exert a degree of self-control. I found a recipe for mastering self-control in Entrepreneur magazine recently, and I will adapt and share that. But first, a quick story to illustrate what self-control looks like in a real-world scenario I experienced firsthand.

I know a great seller and leader named Brian. He has a long history of sales success, and he is currently doing extremely well financially while leading a team in the investment management and advisory business. Brian is a great example of how a sales leader's self-control puts a positive imprint on the conduct of every member of his or her team.

Brian and I once worked together in an environment in which several members of the executive leadership team engaged in what I will describe as less-than-exemplary moral behavior. Workplace affairs and some rather scandalous behavior took place among members of the leadership team, and it was the worst-kept secret in the company. When leaders conduct themselves in this way, I've found that their teams are put in a very uncomfortable position. Should we look the other way? Should we take a stand and say something? Should we mind our own business, or should we acknowledge that certain behavior, particularly in the workplace, destroys trust, lowers morale, and distracts people from their work?

But none of this was true on Brian's team, as we knew that he conducted himself not only with great professionalism but with moderation, temperance, and integrity. Brian was fun to be around, but he wasn't a big partier. He knew how to create an enjoyable environment in which everyone felt valued and safe. He exemplified self-control, and without ever having to say it, he expected the same degree of self-control from members of his team. On his team, we were somewhat insulated from the scandalous behavior of others, and I really appreciated that. Frankly, I didn't have any patience for the philandering executives, and I didn't trust them. I relied on and trusted Brian, and my career flourished while on his team.

The lesson we can learn from Brian is very simple: Demonstrate self-control, and your people will heed your example. They will appreciate the sort of environment you create because that environment is conducive to mutual respect and trust building.

Back to that recipe for self-control that I found in *Entrepreneur* magazine. Deep Patel wrote the piece published in May 2019, titled, "10 Powerful Ways to Master Self-Discipline & Lead A Happier Life." I am a fan of lists, and Patel offers a top ten list. I found most of the items on his list to be pertinent for sales leaders, and the condensed list of items for your consideration follows:

- Know your weaknesses—Take an honest inventory of your weaknesses and acknowledge them. Own up to them, and you can begin to address the vulnerabilities and the situations that might cause you to lose control and to fall to vice.

- Remove temptations—Do yourself the favor of avoiding the things that tempt you. You're human, and you aren't strong enough to overcome every temptation. Like the great prayer tells us, "Lead us not into temptation." That is a direct request to the good Lord for help when temptations arise. Why? Because we can't do it alone!

- Set clear goals and have an execution plan—Perhaps not surprisingly, achieving a higher degree of self-control starts with a clear vision of what you want to achieve and what kind of leader you want your people to have. As Patel suggests, create a mantra to keep yourself focused. Examples include:
  - I am strengthening my self-control every day.
  - Today, I am going to exercise my self-control and enjoy the day to the fullest!
  - I am strong, but I will lean on God when I need more strength today.

- Build your self-discipline—Building self-control can only be achieved through daily diligence. Don't worry about the challenges you'll face tomorrow. Today will be challenging enough!

- Reward yourself—When you have a great day and demonstrate self-control, a little indulgence or reward is appropriate. Just don't be piggish about it!

- Forgive yourself and move forward—If you have a bad day, give yourself a pass. Tomorrow is another day. Self-control hinges on the belief that you are worthy and good enough to live virtuously. Forgive yourself, and when given the opportunity to ask others for forgiveness and to make things right, take it.

At the risk of this chapter devolving into a mini self-help book, it is important to remember the context in which I am defining self-control as a critical and desirable virtue. As sales leaders, our ability to build trust with our people, with clients, and with our peers is paramount to our success. There is a direct link between self-control and our ability to build trust.

As David Maister, Charles Green, and Robert Galford put it in their book, The Trusted Advisor (Touchstone, 2001) the trust equation has three variables that positively affect trust:

1. Credibility

2. Reliability

3. Intimacy

There is one factor that negatively impacts trust—self-orientation. To sum it up, leaders who can achieve some greater degree of self-control will project a low self-orientation to their key constituents. In so doing, they will make a positive impact on the divisor in the trust equation, increasing trust. Put simply, demonstrate self-control, and you will demonstrate a low self-orientation to your team and others. That low self-orientation will increase the degree to which you are trusted by them. (I recommend you read the book from Maister et al or simply look up "Maister's Trust Equation" online for a deep dive into the variables in the equation.)

I acknowledge that the rewards and trappings of success are a big part of our lives as salespeople. All that I am suggesting in this chapter is that we be conscious of the balance between self-control and indulgence. While there is nothing wrong with rewarding ourselves at the right times, being overly indulgent and not keeping our desires in check can lead to really bad things for us and for our teams.

The question is, how do you manifest self-control in an even greater way as you lead? How can you strike a better balance between the natural tendency to indulge your desires and the need to demonstrate self-control to others?

Start, Stop, Continue exercise

What can I do right now to demonstrate self-control with my sellers? With clients? With partners? With my colleagues?
What must I stop doing to avoid demonstrating excessive indulgence in front of my team, my customers, my colleagues?
What should I continue doing to serve as an example of self-control as I work with clients? As I work with partners? As I collaborate with colleagues?

"Detachment, properly understood, means freedom, inner freedom."

—*Albert Nolan*

"The greatest asset to the human experience is the ability to navigate one's emotions. By practicing the skill of detachment, one can successfully step back from the potentially destructive and tune into the purely positive."

—*Gary Hopkins*

Chapter Seven

Lustful Desires and the Ready! Fire! Aim! Sales Culture

Lust in the carnal sense plagues us all, and the use and abuse of others for our own pleasure is a deep and insidious sin. I am not going to address that type of lust in this chapter. In the context of sales, lust takes a different form—an urgent need for results, for action, for busy-ness. The lustful sales leader looks at his or her people like a commodity to be employed for the purpose of immediate results.

Purposeful Urgency

I once knew a sales leader, we'll call him Bernie, whose mantra as a leader was, "We have to act with urgency." It is hard to argue with that sentiment, as moving with urgency is important in the dynamic world of sales. You never know when simply acting faster than your competitor might be the reason you win and they lose.

The trouble with Bernie's brand of urgency, however, was that it wasn't *purposeful urgency*. He tended to move with urgency from one thing to the next without any apparent rationale, and he expected everyone else around him to act in roughly the same manner. I once heard someone describe this as a ***"Ready! Fire! Aim!"*** approach to work. I think that is a good way to describe Bernie's approach. In an effort to move with urgency, he tended to act quickly without necessarily thinking things through. I suppose it was fine for him to work that way, as he had been a reasonably successful seller himself.

The real problem arose when Bernie expected people on his team to act on his priorities and to move with the same type of un-purposeful urgency. His priorities changed so often that it was difficult for his people to understand why they were being asked to do what he wanted. He never slowed down enough to explain the what, why, and how behind his requests for action. Because his expectations were unclear, Bernie's people were essentially set up to fail. They didn't understand how success would be measured for the tasks they were given, nor did they understand why they were being asked to shift their priorities again.

This overriding and urgent desire for action and results created an environment in which sellers were confused about what was expected of them and how they should go about achieving what they were tasked with, and their leader became progressively more frustrated with his team. In his urgent desire for results, Bernie inadvertently created an environment where talented sellers could not succeed and felt like they were failures. Not surprisingly, Bernie's organization suffered severe turnover problems over a period of several years, and to this day, he struggles to build a winning sales organization.

Unfortunately, this story is all too common. In an effort to push a sales team for more sales, a sort of false urgency or extreme pressure is applied. Nothing says, "I don't understand how our buyers buy," quite like a sales leader who sets unrealistic expectations for how quickly deals need to be advanced and won, for example.

To be perfectly clear, I am not railing against the idea of creating a sense of urgency for a sales team. Acting with urgency is important for sellers, but setting unrealistic timelines for seller actions conveys the wrong message. In a nutshell, sellers conclude that they are being set up for failure when their leader demands results in an unrealistic way. The leader who chooses artificial urgency as a motivator tends to achieve the opposite—a demotivated sales team that feels its manager is out of touch with reality.

Detaching from Urgency

Standing opposed to the lust for urgent results, the virtue of detachment is a driver of the sort of behavior that supports effective sales execution. I recently spoke with Mike Kiernan, currently the vice president of sales for North America at Congruent Solutions, about how a former coach and sales leader's detachment from the need for urgent results led to a complete turnaround in Mike's performance as a wholesaler of 401 (k) solutions.

Back in 2014-15, Mike was a wholesaler at AXA Distributors, and he carried an annual sales goal of approximately $16 million. The team Mike was part of was responsible for pursuing independent advisor relationships. This was a brand-new channel, with new strategic partnerships and a new sales team.

Mike shared, "As a wholesaler, you're told you need to see a lot of advisors, so that's what I did." Mike did as he was told. His first year's production was solid, and his results seemed to indicate he was on the right track for a long and successful run with this new channel. Then he plateaued. Despite being very active and visiting with a lot of advisors, his results leveled off in year two.

"The solution wasn't going to be to see more and more people,"

Mike said. "That wasn't fixing the problem." When the results problem persisted, Mike was moved to a new Division Vice President's (DVP) team.

This new DVP noticed that Mike had plateaued in terms of results, despite consistently exceeding his activity and meeting goals.

The DVP told Mike, "I don't want you to go out and see any other advisors." He also told Mike that he would go out into the field with Mike to help him. He wanted Mike to forget what others had told him about activity.

The urgent desire for action was getting in the way. Striving to hit aggressive activity goals was getting in the way of Mike's ability to achieve the results he was paid to achieve.

The need to get more meetings with advisors had overtaken the need to be well-prepared and advisor-centered in his approach. The DVP had to temper his urgent desire for results to ensure that Mike the wholesaler could be as effective as he was required to be.

"I followed his instructions," Mike said. "I postponed meetings with new advisors, and I started rebuilding my territory with the approach my new DVP recommended."

Mike invested more time into planning and critical thinking about his meetings with advisors. He told me about one of his biggest wins at the time, which he attributes to slowing things down and detaching himself from the need for urgent action all the time, per his DVP's advice.

Mike and his DVP sat down together, and they identified a few target advisors that Mike would focus on deeply. They were intentional about how Mike would plan and execute his approach to one of these targeted advisors. Mike carried out the plan methodically.

This particular advisor was gunning for a large piece of insurance business with a family-owned company that was already working with him on its retirement plan. In addition to retaining the 401 (k) plan, this advisor was able to win a significant amount of new insurance business, stealing this away from an incumbent insurance provider who had the relationship for many years.

Mike recalled that he "ended up closing the largest plan that had ever been closed by anyone in our group, roughly a $13 million plan. The deal was with an older advisor who I hadn't worked with before." Mike told me he would not have been able to win this deal if his DVP had continued pressing him for immediate activity and improvement in results.

"My DVP had me slow things down to focus in on having quality meetings," he said. The DVP worked with Mike on exactly how each conversation needed to be constructed and executed. His message: be thorough and intentional in everything that you do.

Then came another win, and another . . . and Mike finished third out of twenty-five wholesalers despite a somewhat rough start to his second year with the company. Mike finished the year with approximately $24 million won against a goal of $16 million that year.

Mike's advice based on what he learned is, "Plan before you execute. Don't just rush out into the field and be active." Don't let the urgent desire for activity supersede the need to be effective at each and every interaction.

The DVP's guidance: "Don't just take marching orders and get out into the field for the sake of being active." Stop and think about how to make those activities more likely to produce a good outcome.

What can we learn from the example set by Mike and his DVP? I think the main lesson is we have to strike a balance between the need for urgency and the need to be purposeful and effective.

I categorized detachment as one of the "other-oriented" virtues, and I did so because this virtue constrains us from putting pressure on others to give us results that they cannot deliver urgently. Instead, a leader's willingness to detach himself or herself from the urgent puts people on his or her team in a position to seek first what is most important, which may be clarity or a better plan to get the result they want. Detachment from the need for urgent results gives a team the space and time it needs to be effective.

As you consider your own attachment to urgency, do you have room for improvement? Are there situations where the sort of purposeful detachment that Mike's DVP demonstrated would lead to a better result than if you were to press for urgent but un-purposeful action?

If the answer to those questions is yes, then complete the Start, Stop, Continue exercise to commit to some small changes you can make now.

Start, Stop, Continue exercise

What can I do right now to constructively demonstrate detachment with my team?
What must I stop doing to avoid acting with un-purposeful urgency? What must I stop doing to discourage my team acting with urgency for urgency's sake alone?
What should I continue doing to act with appropriate urgency? What should I continue doing to ensure the right balance between urgency and thoughtfulness with my team?

"Habits form virtues—powers of your soul that help you enjoy the goodness of life. Again: virtues are power."

—*Chris Stefanick*

Chapter Eight

Applying the Great Virtues to Sales Leadership

As you read the stories about virtuous sales leaders in this book, a reasonable conclusion would be, "I need to commit to strengthening one virtue that really resonated with me." That would be a great thing, and that is one of the key conclusions that I hope you will draw.

But I believe we should push this idea a little further. While I am a strong advocate for focus and making one important change at a time, I think we have to aspire to make bigger changes, bigger improvements to how we do the work of sales leadership.

When we consider the impact of the virtues on the morale, enthusiasm, effort, and ultimately, the results of our teams, we recognize that the more virtuous we can be, the more successful we become—not just based on key performance indicators but on the other, really important indicators of success like job satisfaction, retention, development, and personal success. In every environment where I've seen improvement in the application of one of the virtues, I've noticed a general lift that inspired and created momentum toward something far greater than the team may have believed possible before.

Establishing the Virtuous Circle

If you are not already familiar with the concept of the Virtuous Circle, the following definition from *The Merriam-Webster Dictionary* will help:

> **Virtuous Circle (n):** a chain of events in which one desirable occurrence leads to another which further promotes the first occurrence and so on resulting in a continuous process of improvement

I found an interesting example of how the virtuous circle plays out in modern, professional sales while interviewing a few people who are featured in this book. Julia Flohr's story is about the impact of a sales leader's diligence on her team. Dana Isola's story is about how humility changed the way he leads and performs his job. Their stories highlight two different virtues, but the environments they created had the same hallmark. They both created environments in which sellers put in their absolute best effort, working exceptionally hard but doing so in a very positive, enthusiastic way. Both Dana and Julia said their teams put in maximum effort, but they also said they had fun doing so. What sales leader would not want that from his or her team?

As Dana Isola puts it, "I don't want to take their joy away," speaking about reps and how a manager can affect the degree to which they take enjoyment, personal motivation, and positive energy from their work.

I hope that you've experienced that sort of working environment in your career at least once, where enthusiasm, hard work, fun, and a focus on getting better every day are the rule and not the exception. I've been fortunate enough to work in that type of environment more than once. It is a sales leader's choice to incorporate a more virtuous approach to her or his job that leads to this kind of positive and affirming environment.

Why?

When sellers witness or experience virtuous behavior from their leader firsthand, they know that they are valued. Following are the messages they receive:

- When I demonstrate humility, I show you that our working relationship isn't about me. It is about you.

- When I show gratitude for your effort or extend goodwill to you even when I don't have to, I am telling you I value you.

- When I am patient with you, even in times when you are trying my patience, I am showing you I understand how challenging this work is.

- When I am lively and diligent at my work, I am offering an example that will inspire you.

- When I am generous with my time or with my resources, I am demonstrating that you matter.

- When I exhibit self-control, I am showing you that I refuse to put my needs and my emotions first.

- When I demonstrate detachment from the need for immediate results, I am encouraging you to be deliberate and to apply your God-given talents and strengths to get the work done in the most effective way you can.

All of this, in a nutshell, leads to a very important conclusion in the seller's mind: My leader genuinely cares about me. I am not some organ grinder's monkey, racing around for the coins that motivate me. I am fearfully, wonderfully made, and my leader treats me accordingly.

Are there sellers who might take advantage of the virtuous sales leader's generosity, patience, diligence, goodwill, or detachment? Unfortunately, yes. When they do, those who would take advantage can do real damage to the esprit de corps of a virtuous sales leader's team. But they also stick out like a sore thumb. The types of sellers who would take advantage of a leader's good graces ultimately will not fit in to the team, as the other sellers who give more effort, who support one another, who take a positive, enthusiastic approach to overcoming barriers to success simply will not tolerate a member of the team who doesn't contribute in a positive way.

I'm reminded of a situation many years ago when I was a seller on a team selling to large enterprises. It was a talented group of people, and we all carried big quotas, worked hard, and put in a lot of effort. There was one member of our team, however, who was downright abusive to people down and up the command chain. She treated everyone poorly, and she had a long line of project managers and support people who left the company because of the way she treated them. She treated our boss like a dog, too. She would say openly how he was of no use to her, and the only value he delivered for her was to get exceptions made from time to time that helped her get her job done. I never understood why people tolerated her behavior, but it wasn't really my problem at the time. As for the rest of the people on our team, they had little respect for her, and they would not help her in situations when she asked for their help. She hung on with the company for quite a while, but in the end, she had so few allies that she had no choice but to leave. Despite nearly a decade of high performance, she left without even as much as a happy hour to say goodbye. She had worn out her welcome.

You may be thinking while reading this, "Why didn't her boss get rid of her if she was such a bear?" It's a great question, and I confess I don't know the answer. The story illustrates not only what can happen to someone who takes advantages of the leader's good graces, it also shows that even the most virtuous leader needs to draw a line in the sand at times. We cannot expect our virtuous choices and behavior to keep every bad actor or poor performer in line. But that is not really why we should choose to be more virtuous in our approach to sales leadership. We don't build organizations worrying about whether one bad apple will spoil the culture and kill the esprit de corps. We build the best team or organization we can, knowing that bad actors and poor performers ultimately will not fit in. That may be the best we can do, and we cannot worry about being taken advantage of when we choose first to be virtuous sales leaders.

"We are what we repeatedly do. Excellence, then, is not an act but a habit."

— *Aristotle*

Chapter Nine

Practice, Practice, Practice: Committing to the Virtues, Avoiding the Deadly Sins

You've read stories about virtuous leaders who have accomplished great things, and my hope is that these stories have inspired you to commit more deeply to one or more of the virtues in your professional life and perhaps beyond. The Start, Stop, Continue exercise at the end of each chapter is there to enable you to think practically about how to incorporate more virtuous behavior in your daily work with your team. Conceiving of the changes you'll need to make may have been relatively simple.

You might have also had the thought that approaching your work in a more virtuous way is going to be difficult. You're right. Living and leading with a deeper commitment to the great virtues is difficult.

Is it any more difficult than becoming a great golfer or a pianist or sculptor? Is there any less commitment required to becoming a virtuoso in other vocations? I think not. Anything that can give

115

you great satisfaction, like becoming the type of leader who leads sales teams to great heights consistently, is going to require hard work. Don't be discouraged. I presume you are in the role you are today because you have been willing to put in the work that others were not.

Speaking from personal experience, the payoff of consciously choosing to avoid undesirable behavior and to choose virtue is immense. The feelings that I have on my best, most virtuous days include joy, self-assurance, confidence, and excitement for what is to come. That makes it possible for me to radiate confidence, good humor, and enthusiasm out to my team. How do you feel on those days when you are at your best, your most virtuous? How does your team react on those *best days*?

We want more of that feeling, don't we?

If we are going to be really contemplative right now, we also have to reflect on our own undesirable behavior and how it affects us and the people around us. I can easily recall the feeling that accompanies my own sinful, undesirable behavior. Without anyone else needing to make me feel this way, I feel guilty and less confident, and I'm certainly not joyful. These feelings are real, they're powerful, and they stem naturally from our experience. The thing about being less virtuous and more sinful is that it creates a vicious cycle, the opposite of the virtuous circle we talked about earlier in this book. The vicious cycle in this case looks like this:

- Start seeing yourself as a sinful human, and you'll tend toward sinning—after all, it's who you've come to believe you are . . . as a leader, as a seller, as a member of a team.

- Start seeing yourself as a virtuous human, and you'll tend toward virtue and away from sin. This is how the topic of mindset crosses paths with the seven deadly sins. There is a choice to be made—will you be a virtuous sales leader, or will you be one who tends toward the seven deadly sins and who struggles to find a way out?

The Power of Virtues

Chris Stefanick is an internationally acclaimed author, speaker, and TV show host. In a recent blog, he wrote, "Habits form virtues— powers of your soul that help you enjoy the goodness of life. Again: virtues are power."

If any part of what I've written about the seven deadly sins or about how to be a more virtuous sales leader feels like I am recommending you make yourself weak or give up power, you may be misreading this book. Being virtuous is being powerful. Virtuousness leads to greater followership, motivation, and enthusiasm among your team. You will still have to pay attention to talent, process, time and effort management, and all the things that sales leadership typically entails, but virtuous leadership makes all of that more enjoyable, more motivating, and ultimately, more effective.

"Habits form virtues—powers of your soul that help you enjoy the goodness of life. Again: virtues are power."

—*Chris Stefanick*

What virtues can you increase by committing to new habits? What "powers of your soul" can you further develop that will contribute to greater joy not only in your own life but in the lives of the people you work with every day?

Having experienced both sides of this sin-versus-virtue dynamic personally, I will never go back to the mode in which selfish, sinful behavior is the hallmark of my work. The joy I have derived from my work over the last several years by approaching it in an intentionally virtuous way radiates throughout my work. Those closest to me will tell you that I am naturally reserved, at times quiet, and worse, brooding and prone to the occasional down-cycle. I have to work at positivity, but having experienced the joy that comes directly from a virtuous approach to work and the rest of my life, I recommit each and every day to a more virtuous approach to work and to developing others. I have concluded that is actually my natural orientation, my default position, as I am more confident and effective when being intentionally more virtuous.

I told the story about Dana Isola in Chapter One of this book, and I want to relay to you the impact that being intentionally more virtuous has had on his career since the day he fully and really committed to the virtue of humility. That virtue has become his hallmark. Everyone I have met who worked for or with Dana over the last few years says the same things . . . fantastic seller, inspiring leader, wonderful person, great coach, "I'd follow him anywhere."

From the moment that he committed to practicing humility, everything changed for Dana. Seemingly all at once, Dana was given practically unlimited opportunities, participating in corporate initiatives, flying all over the country to talk with teams, helping to coach underperforming reps in other regions. Dana has become an important and positive force within the Medtronic sales organization. He applied the virtue of humility to his daily work and to his relationships with others, and the impact on his career trajectory and personal satisfaction was enormous and practically immediate. A long line of people from his team have been promoted into various positions of responsibility, and I expect he will continue to build upon that long line of skilled and dedicated sellers who will benefit directly from his approach to leadership.

I hope that you will make a similar choice and that you get to experience the joy, the strengthening of the "powers of your soul" that will propel you to great success—however you define success for yourself and those around you.

Chapter Ten

A Final Word of Encouragement

As I've said in my two previous books, the choice to be excellent is yours to make. We've just explored what happens when people who lead sales organizations choose to adopt the great virtues and reject the seven deadly sins. Based on what I've experienced through my own work and by observing the work of others, the evidence is clear. Leaders who make the effort to adopt and practice the great virtues build and sustain great teams that can weather the ups and downs of modern business.

The stories I've shared throughout this book serve as evidence of the correlation between the application of the great virtues and sales leadership effectiveness. This correlation exists in the context of sales leadership because, at its core, sales leadership rises and falls on our ability to build strong, enduring relationships with sellers, with clients, with colleagues, and with partners.

A very wise man I once knew and who left us too soon, Monsignor

Thomas Wells, once told me, "The only thing that can come between you and your wife is sin." He said this in the context of a very deep and important conversation early in my marriage to Sandy (with whom I just celebrated twenty-five years of marriage). You may be wondering, "How is this relevant to the subject of sales leadership?"

I could cite quite a few examples from the last couple of decades in which my choices of vice over virtue led to an argument or a division in the most important human relationship I have. When I choose vice over virtue, my relationships falter. The correlation between sinful choices and negative impact on relationships is real. I imagine you've experienced the impact of sin in a similar way on your relationships, both personal and professional.

Deadly Sins, Deadly Consequences

To bring this point full circle and back into the realm of professional selling, I will offer another story from the real-world. This story is deeply personal, and I will offer a very brief version of it. If you would like to read a complete and very well-researched version of the story, pick up a copy of the book, *Poison Pills: The Untold Story of the Vioxx Drug Scandal,* by Tom Nesi (Thomas Dunne Books, 2008).

The publisher's summary of the book offers the following background:

> To the millions of Americans who suffer from chronic pain and arthritis, Vioxx seemed like a miracle. One of the most widely promoted and prescribed pain medications in the world—used by more than twenty million people—it was endorsed by the medical establishment and celebrities such as Olympic champion figure skater Dorothy Hamill. With annual sales of $2.5 billion, Vioxx became a pharmaceutical bonanza before

being abruptly taken off the market in September 2004, after it was revealed that it led to an increased risk of heart-related disease and death.

Drawing on internal documents, video footage, court testimony, and exclusive interviews, as well as three decades of experience inside the medical industry, Tom Nesi tells the dramatic story of what the drug's manufacturer, Merck, knew and when. It is a compelling narrative of business and medical science run amok, with a cast of characters ranging from those at the highest levels of the multibillion-dollar pharmaceutical industry to research scientists, marketers, and drug company sales reps. Here also are accounts from physicians, lawyers, financial analysts, and patients and their families whose lives have been forever altered by Vioxx.

The parts of Nesi's compelling narrative in *Poison Pills* that are most relevant to me and to the theme of this book center on the drug company sales reps, a physician, and a single patient and his family.

The sales reps in this story engaged in selling practices that were dubious professionally. Their selling practices are well documented in Nesi's book, and the tactics those sellers were encouraged to apply in sales calls with prescribers were shockingly manipulative and not patient focused.

Without knowing the exact, personal motivation of every sales manager at Merck who encouraged the wrong behavior at the expense of doctors and patients, we can point to several of the deadly sins as a likely culprit and contributing factor that led to the horribly ineffective sales leadership described in Nesi's book.

Was it pride that led those sales managers to encourage reps to go out and win new prescribers at all costs? Was greed the driver of their behavior? Were they lazy about how they addressed some of the legitimate concerns that prescribers and patients had about their product, choosing to dodge questions and concerns instead of working to understand and address them? Were they so piggish and self-indulgent that they didn't even worry about the negative effects of their behavior on doctors and patients?

My guess is that it was probably some or all of those specific sins that were at play in the *Poison Pills* saga. The reason that story is so relevant to me may surprise you. It is not simply because the Vioxx scandal was such a big story that has obvious implications for how drug marketing and selling are done forever. This story is relevant because I know fully the impact of sin-filled sales leadership not only on pharmaceutical sellers but on doctors and patients. One of those doctors, highly reputable and respected, fully believed in the product that he prescribed to his patients. He did so because he trusted the sales team who called on him. He trusted them so much that he prescribed the drug to an elderly patient who ultimately and unfortunately suffered a heart attack and a debilitating injury that affected the remaining years of his life. That patient eventually died of congestive heart failure.

As you can imagine, the doctor in this story must have assumed that the drug reps who called on him had his and his patients' best interests at heart. You can also imagine how he must have felt when he learned about the choices the drug company and its sales organization made that led to such a terrible outcome. Suffice it to say that he would refuse to do business with that organization again, and we can understand why.

The patient I referenced was my father, John G. McDarby.

If you could have known my father, one of his hallmarks, one of his great strengths was his integrity. He made a good living as a seller and sales leader, certainly enough to pay for the care and feeding of his wife and five children in the New York metropolitan area. He wasn't perfect, but he would never have deceived anyone to make a sale or encouraged any of the dozens of salespeople he supervised over his nearly fifty-year commercial insurance sales career to do so. The great irony of the *Poison Pills* saga is that the life of an honorable salesman was so terribly impacted by the less-than-honorable actions of sellers and their leaders. It didn't have to be that way. Someone could have made different choices. Some sales leader could have called out the sinful behavior, and perhaps some or all of the terrible consequences for patients, for doctors, for salespeople, for leaders, and for the entire Merck organization could have been avoided.

In the extreme example we find in the *Poison Pills* story, the consequences were literally deadly. In addition to the impact on doctors and patients, Merck lost billions of dollars, and forfeited an immeasurable amount of goodwill and trust. I wonder how things would have been different if someone in sales leadership had taken action—pointing out the pridefulness, or the avarice, or the lust for results at all costs—and put a stop to the wrong behavior. Could the whole Vioxx disaster have been avoided? Could the degree to which doctors and patients trusted Merck have been preserved or even improved?

To be perfectly clear, I need to point out that there are great sales leaders in the biopharmaceutical industry. I know there are because I work with some of them. They set an expectation with their sales teams that they will "first, do no harm," and they demonstrate humility, goodwill, patience, diligence, and self-control as they lead. Their sellers build trust, create value, and establish strong and enduring relationships with prescribers. The same is true in every business-to-business segment that I've come across. There are some bad actors in sales leadership, and there are some truly inspirational leaders ... hopefully more of the latter than the former. And then there are a whole lot of us who live in between. We're not as virtuous and strong as we could be as leaders, and our performance is diminished, our teams led at times astray.

The moral that connects the *Poison Pills* story with this book is simply this—if you want to really and truly lead (sales)people to greatness, then you must take steps to be the most virtuous leader you can be today. You must actively avoid the seven deadly sins as a sales leader, or you risk some serious consequences, including the erosion of trust, the diminishment of the value you create for others, and the destruction of relationships—with buyers, with your team, with your colleagues, and with your partners.

How do the deadly sins erode trust? Trust remains the number-one, most important differentiator in business-to-business sales (according to my own primary research, published in the advisory brief titled, "The New Definition of Value" [2015 edition], and referenced in *The Cadence of Excellence*). For buyers who are willing to make purchasing decisions based on criteria other than price, trust is far and away the decision-making criterion that tips the scales in favor of one seller over another most often. If you and your team demonstrate any of the seven deadly sins during your interactions with customers, you will erode trust. Count on it.

How do the deadly sins diminish the value we create? In today's context, buyers value how we interact with them far more than what we sell them. They want us to help them gain insight into their issues and opportunities, identify new ways to get the outcomes they desire, and broker the resources we have access to, to help them achieve what they need. Demonstrating virtues such as humility, goodwill, and diligence goes hand-in-glove with the type of behavior that buyers value and expect today. Demonstrating sinful behavior diminishes our ability to create value for others.

How do the deadly sins destroy relationships? At the core of human relationships lies trust and willing the good of the other.

Put another way, trust and love are critical to building and strengthening relationships. The virtues are manifestations of love, but the deadly sins manifest the opposite.

These are consequences that all of us in sales would like to avoid without a doubt.

It is a challenge to be less sinful and more virtuous, and speaking from experience, the only way you can rise to the challenge is daily. If you had a bad day yesterday and you're embarrassed by the choices you made as a leader, don't brood over it. Get back to the work of being a more virtuous leader now, following the examples of the people I've told you about in this book and those virtuous leaders you've experienced directly in your career. It isn't too late.

If you had a great day yesterday, full of virtuous actions and other-focused decisions that led to great outcomes for your people, your clients, your colleagues, and your loved ones, then I have a few suggestions for you, as well. First, remember how you feel right now. Do you feel a certain inner strength, a certain confidence about how you are going about your work? That is a direct effect of your choice to take the virtuous path toward your goals. Being more virtuous leads us all to feel more fully ourselves, more of who we are really meant to be. You were made for virtue, not sin.

Second, don't let your guard down. There are real forces at work in this world that pull us toward sin and sinful behavior. You can't expect denial or modern forms of rationalization or relativism to make them go away. Be ready to battle with those forces again tomorrow.

Finally, remember that it is the combination of the virtues and not simply focusing on one of them that will bring about the most positive and enduring impact on your professional and personal life. For instance, if you are naturally humble and maintain strong self-control, then perhaps you can find a way to incorporate more gratitude or generosity in the way you lead. If you are very good at demonstrating patience and a certain detachment from immediate results, then perhaps a little bit more liveliness and diligence are in order. Even the most virtuous leader has something he or she needs to work on to advance to the next stage of leadership excellence.

Which virtues have you decided to focus on next? What actions will you take to become a more virtuous leader starting right now?

Make your choice today, and act upon it.

One Last Story and a Prayer to the Patron Saint of Salespeople

Yes, there is a patron saint of salespeople in the Catholic Christian tradition. She is Saint Lucy. Saint Lucy's Feast Day is December 13, which also happens to be my father's birthday.

The rumor has it that Lucy was such a popular saint in the medieval church that many groups claimed her as their patron. Salespeople may claim Lucy as their patron saint for any number of reasons, but one explanation I read claims that Lucy's dowry (inheritance) was to be distributed among the poor, requiring someone to go door-to-door to locate who needed the most help. While that is not exactly what the modern sales trade looks like today, we sellers do a lot of knocking and a lot of helping. That may be reason enough for us to honor Saint Lucy today.

Lucy earned her reputation as a brave and godly woman by overcoming obstacle after obstacle, and her legendary status stands the test of time. She lived in the early fourth century, and we remember her even now because of her great faithfulness and courage. She died for her faith, and while she lived, she persisted at praying and petitioning her mother to allow her to serve Christ and the church rather than marrying. Apparently, her persuasiveness is also a contributing factor to her selection as the patron saint of salespeople.

In addition to being the patron saint of salespeople, Saint Lucy is known as the patron saint of blindness and of those suffering from eye diseases. Why? Because, like so many other stories of heroic saints, Lucy's story ended in a torturous death—a death that included her eyes being plucked out. Apparently, the Roman governor of the time was not such a great fan of Lucy's virtuousness.

To dwell on how Lucy died would miss the point. She committed her life to virtue, and while we don't have to worry today about being put to death by the governor or having our eyes plucked out, we should focus our energy on how we go about leading the people in our charge.

If you pray, let us pray for a great deal more virtue and a lot less sin in our professional and personal lives. The following is a prayer to Saint Lucy:

"O God, our Creator and Redeemer, mercifully hear our prayers that as we venerate your servant, Saint Lucy, for the light of faith you bestowed upon her, you would increase and preserve this same light in our souls that we may be able to avoid evil, to do good, and to abhor nothing so much as the blindness and the darkness of evil and of sin. Relying on your goodness, O God, we humbly ask you, by the intercessory prayers of your servant, Saint Lucy, that you would give perfect vision to our eyes, that they may serve for your greater honor and glory and for the salvation of our souls in this world, that we may come to the enjoyment of your unfailing light of the Lamb of God in paradise. Saint Lucy, virgin and martyr, hear our prayers and obtain our petitions. Amen!"

Appendix: Recommended Reading List

If you enjoyed this look at how the great virtues can positively affect your professional and personal life, I recommend that you invest some of your future reading time into other books that dwell deeply and differently into the virtues.

We each have personal preferences for book genres, book length, and writing style. There are a great many books on virtuousness and the links between the virtues and organizational health, and they range from secular nonfiction works to spiritual guides to religious allegory. Pick one or a few of them up. They can help you on the next steps of your journey to being a more virtuous leader and help you to educate and encourage others to do the same.

My personal book recommendations on the virtues include the following:

- *The Screwtape Letters*, by C. S. Lewis (or virtually anything by Lewis!)
  Lewis is perhaps best known as the author of *The Chronicles of Narnia,* and he is one of my personal favorites. He wrote this incredible and unique religious satire, told from the vantage point of a demon named Screwtape. The story details the various attempts of Satan's demons to tempt and capture the soul of one particular human. Ultimately, the story is about man's triumph over temptation and evil. *The Screwtape Letters* is at once serious in tone but also legitimately entertaining and funny.

- *The Book of Virtues*, by William Bennett
  This anthology contains stories plucked from American history, the Bible, Greek mythology, and various works of fiction and poetry. Each story illustrates the virtues that we aspire to live out and want to teach others. It's a great

piece to add to your collection, especially if you have the occasion to pass on the stories to children or others who are looking for inspiration to overcome vices.

- *Seven Deadly Sins, Seven Lively Virtues Study Guide*, by Bishop Robert Barron
One of the great Christian teachers and apologists of our time, Bishop Barron shows us how to oppose the seven deadly sins consciously and practically, setting ourselves on the path to peace and joy by applying the lively virtues. The guide is available at the Word On Fire website.

- *The Bad Catholic's Guide to the Seven Deadly Sins,* by John Zmirak
You can probably tell by my recommendation of C. S. Lewis and this installment from the "Bad Catholic's Guides" that I like my theology and religious educational content with a healthy dose of humor. Zmirak combines insights from history and theology with stories and a few quizzes to help readers test their virtuousness. If you want to have some fun while digging deeper into how to avoid the seven deadly sins in your work and personal life, pick up this guide.

Other Books by Matthew McDarby

The Cadence of Excellence: Key Habits of Effective Sales Managers

The Ultimate Differentiator: The Sales Manager's Guide to Talent Development.

Available on Amazon

About the Author

Matthew McDarby is a sales leadership coach and advisor to some of the world's best run sales forces, and he is the founder and President of United Sales Resources.

In addition to leading his company's sales effort, he leads the company's research and advisory team. Prior to founding his own company, Matt served as the vice president of enterprise sales for Huthwaite, one of the world's leading sales training companies and creators of SPIN Selling. Before joining Huthwaite, he worked in sales, sales management, and consulting roles in the technology and professional services industries in the New York and Washington, D.C., metropolitan areas.

Matt has coached and advised hundreds of sales leaders and their salesforces in a wide range of industries, helping them win new business and create value for their clients. He has written or co-authored dozens of white papers, advisory briefs, and e-books on the subjects of sales excellence and sales leadership, and he frequently facilitates workshops to help salespeople and leaders gain a competitive edge in complex business-to-business sales.

Matt and his wife, Sandy, have four children and reside in the Washington, D.C., area. He is an active community, church, and youth sports volunteer, and he is a fanatical New York Giants fan.

Best ways to reach Matt:
LinkedIn: www.linkedin.com/in/mattmcdarby
Company website: www.usr-llc.com
Email: matt@usr-llc.com
Twitter: @mmcdarby
Instagram: @mattmcdarby1970

Made in the USA
Coppell, TX
13 October 2021